Grammar
Essentials

Geoff Barton

LONGMAN

CONTENTS

INTRODUCTION

SECTION 2 CLAUSES AND PHRASES:
Creating islands of words

SECTION 3 WORD CLASSES:
Using language more precisely

SECTION 4 DISCOURSE STRUCTURE:
Organising whole texts

SECTION 5 PUNCTUATION:
Helping the reader to follow your ideas

* = activities designed for more able students

WHO THIS BOOK IS AIMED AT

My starting point in writing *Grammar Essentials* was simple. Some of the students I have most enjoyed teaching have been lively, funny and really interested in English. They have often been confident in speaking, good at class discussion, and quick to tell me their ideas and opinions.

But when I ask them to write, things sometimes seem to fall apart. Their ideas might be original and interesting, but their writing is hard to follow. One sentence shunts unexpectedly into the next and words seem to tumble endlessly down the page without a sense of control and suddenly it's not clear where one idea starts and the next ends so there's a feeling that we're never going to reach the end and we just keep going on and on like this ...

The result? These students feel that they are failures at writing. They get frustrated. Most keep on trying, but a few just give up. "I'm no good at English," they say. This book is for them – and, if that description sounds familiar, for you too. It aims to teach one essential skill: how to write sentences which are clear, accurate, varied and will add interest to your writing.

HOW THE BOOK IS ORGANISED TO HELP YOU

Each of the book's five sections begins with a list of **aims**, which is designed to show you what you will learn in the section. It will help you to know where you are heading.

Next there are the **units**, each on a different topic. They always begin with an objective: what you are intended to learn from the unit. You are then introduced to the unit's key ideas and are given practice in trying them out. There are between one and three different activities in each unit, the last one usually being more open-ended.

These **activities** are not too lengthy. No one wants to grind through page after page of exercises. But in order to understand an idea, you need to practise it a few times. This is the only way to get a language skill into your bloodstream. The activities will help you to do this.

Answer Page symbol:

The activities are often accompanied by an **Answer Page** symbol, like the one here. This indicates that answers to the activities are suggested in the Homework File.

One unit is often followed by another on a similar theme. This may take the skill you have just worked on and put it into a context – for example, looking at the way different types of sentences work in different types of texts. These context units are an important part of the book. They show that language skills do not exist in isolation, but have an effect and a purpose.

At the end of each section there is a **self-assessment test**. This is your chance to pull your language together and look at the progress you are making. The **glossary** at the end of the book makes it easy to look up the important new grammar words you come across.

HOW THE HOMEWORK FILE FITS IN

The Student Book is accompanied by a **Homework File**. For each unit in the Student Book, there is at least one photocopiable sheet in the Homework File (called a **Copymaster**). This is designed to give you more practice at home, to help you really get to grips with the topics in the Student Book, and to let you explore further the way language works.

Some units have two photocopiable sheets, one straightforward and one more demanding. A few sheets are even designed to let you look at a related topic on your own. Your teacher will guide you to the sheets which will best suit you.

The Homework File contains a **progress chart** for each section you complete in the Student Book. This allows you to make a note of your scores as you go along, so that you can see the areas in which you have really succeeded and those that need more practice. There are also some **practice tests**, so that you can monitor your ability to show your grammatical knowledge in timed conditions.

CONCLUSION

I am grateful to the fourteen students and the team of teachers across the country who helped me to write this book. In testing it for me, and telling me what worked and what didn't, they helped me come to the conclusion that a very systematic approach to teaching the workings of grammar brings confidence and then competence.

Grammar Essentials is a systematic project aiming to show you what grammar is, to develop your skills in its essential areas, and to give you resources to make you feel that you are making solid progress.

The fourteen students have all made huge progress, and are now writing more clearly and with greater control. I hope *Grammar Essentials* helps you make progress too, by showing you what grammar is about and how it can help you to improve your writing skills.

GEOFF BARTON

Sentences:
Organising your ideas clearly

AIMS:

★ to understand the way sentences work

★ to help you to write more accurately and clearly

In this section you will:

★ explore why we use sentences to communicate clearly

★ discover why the sentence is the most important part of grammar

★ learn about two essential ingredients of sentences – the subject and the verb

★ learn to use different sentence styles – simple, compound and complex – in order to add greater variety to your own writing.

Remember:

★ the Homework File has activity sheets so that you can practise all the skills you learn – including exploring statements, questions, commands and exclamations

★ there is a self-assessment test at the end of the section, so you can chart your progress.

1 The language of space aliens

A ALIEN DICTIONARY

Imagine that an alien from outer space is heading towards Earth. It hopes to find out more about what life is like on our planet. It has learnt a few English words – around 50.

Look at the list of words below. Use this as your starting point to come up with the 50 essential words in English the alien might need. You can keep some of the words in the list, or you can replace them with words which you think are more important.

Remember that the alien is going to try to communicate using these words, so choose them carefully. Think of the kinds of things someone new to Planet Earth might want to say.

In pairs, add another 20 words which the alien might need to communicate in basic English.

30 ESSENTIAL WORDS IN ENGLISH		
1 ME	11 UP	21 HOT
2 YOU	12 DOWN	22 WANT
3 HERE	13 THINK	23 MOVE
4 THERE	14 HOME	24 WHERE
5 GOOD	15 LOOK	25 OUT
6 LIKE	16 PLEASE	26 IN
7 EAT	17 NO	27 THE
8 BUILDING	18 FOOD	28 A
9 CAR	19 ANIMAL	29 HAPPY
10 FORWARD	20 PERSON	30 PLACE

B SORTING WORDS

Once you have your collection of important words, sort them out into rough groups:

★ use a red pen or crayon to highlight all the words that describe <u>doing</u> something (walk, eat, and so on) – these are **verbs**

★ use a blue pen or crayon to highlight all the words that <u>name</u> things (building, animal) – these are **nouns**

★ leave all the other words as they are.

C ALIEN-SPEAK!

Now look at the ten sentences on the Alien-speak sheet (in the Homework File) and try using your 50 words to communicate their meanings. Place a capital letter at the start and a full stop at the end and try to make them as clear to understand as possible.

Follow-on : Write a few sentences saying which words in your list were *most* useful and which were *least* useful. Which categories of words did you find most useful – doing? naming? others? Which would you now say are the really essential 5–10 words in English?

> **Key point –** We use words to communicate meanings.
> To make sense, we put the words together to create sentences.

2 What is grammar?

A   SENTENCE GRAMMAR

Do you know what grammar is? Of course you do – you have been using grammar since you were around two years old. After you started using single words ('mama', 'juice'), you began putting words together ('daddy juice', 'big car'). Putting words together – this is the beginning of grammar.

The most important part of grammar is the **sentence**. We use sentences to tell people what we think, what we want, how we are feeling. The sentence is the way we group our ideas together so that they make sense to our reader or listener.

A simple way to describe a sentence would be: 'a group of words that make sense on their own'. So ...

★ **these <u>are</u> sentences:**

The flea bit my kneecap.

I love to eat dog-biscuits.

I sneezed.

The river ran between the high mountains.

★ **and these are <u>not</u> sentences:**

My kneecap.

To eat dog-biscuits.

Sneezed.

Between the high mountains.

They all look like sentences because each begins with a capital letter and ends with a full stop. But only the first group really make complete sense.

Work out which of the following examples are sentences (✔) and which are not (✗). They are all on the subject of giraffes:

1 Giraffes have very good.
2 A giraffe's tongue can be up to 40 centimetres long.
3 Some giraffes might.
4 Giraffes can see things up to half a mile away.
5 A giraffe called George.
6 A Giraffe called George lived at Chester Zoo.

Compare your answers with a friend's. Check the right answers. Write your score out of six on the progress chart.

B JUMBLED SENTENCES

This time it is a bit more tricky to work out whether these are sentences or not. They are all on different topics and the word order has been jumbled up. For each one:

★ put the words into the right order, so that they make sense

★ make sure you have a capital letter at the beginning and a full stop at the end.

1 I chips like

2 the crying baby

3 a rat is there my in house

4 climb tree saw I you that

5 motorcycling was underwater granny

6 dangerous is potholes climbing down

7 after shotgun the fired was she

8 without they the not will into you let a tie restaurant

 Some may have more than one possible order. Write down the one you think works best. Check the answers and write down your score.

Follow-on : Make up five tricky sentences of your own. Jumble them up and use them to test a friend.

> **Key point** – Grammar means putting words together so that they make sense. We learn to do this from an early age. The most important part of grammar is the sentence.

3 Sentence-spotting

A TEXT-MATCHING

There are hundreds of types of written texts. In the box is a short list of just a few.

NEWSPAPERS	ENCYCLOPAEDIAS
BIOGRAPHIES	POETRY
HOLIDAY BROCHURES	CD-ROMS
LEAFLETS	GHOST STORIES
ROMANTIC FICTION	SHOPPING LISTS
NOVELS	

Most of them use sentences (though a shopping list, for example, may not). In the exercise below, see if you can spot the type of text from its sentences. Can you match up extracts 1–6 with their other halves, A–F?

You should:

★ match up the two parts

★ say what type of text they are from.

Draw a table like the one on the left to help you.

TEXT...	MATCHES WITH	TYPE OF TEXT (EG. NOVEL, ENCYCLOPAEDIA, LETTER)
1		
2		
3		
4		
5		
6		

1 Once upon a time ...

2 When the butter has melted ...

3 Although the first computer in the world filled a room ...

4 Exploding in anger, fury unleashed, ...

5 Don't forget to get ...

6 Mary Pickford was born in 1893 and ...

A ... no one guessed then that she would become so famous.

B ... I felt the terrible bitterness burn deeper as time slipped on.

C ... the cheese and catfood.

D ... the space it would need nowadays is the size of a full stop.

E ... an old woman lived deep in the forest.

F ... add a scooped teaspoon of brown sugar.

Compare your answers with a friend's. Note your score on the progress chart.

Then think about this: which of these texts were easiest to match and which were most difficult? Try to say why.

B | MIND THE GAP

Look at these mystery texts. Many of the really important words carrying information ('lexical' words) have been removed. See if you can still work out what type of text each is.

Mystery text 1

When I was a child I had a very frightening _____. I must have been around five at the _____. It all _____ when I woke up.

Mystery text 2

Once you have _____ all the _____ together, put them aside in a large _____. They will need about 25 _____ for all the flavours to _____. Whilst waiting, _____ the _____. Start by finely _____ the _____ and putting them in a _____ of boiling _____.

Mystery text 3

_____ Sara, I am writing to _____ you to my _____. It will take _____ on _____ 23rd July at 5.30pm. I _____ that you will be _____ to _____.

Follow-on : Copy the first paragraph from a leaflet or book – for example, a novel, encyclopaedia or cookery book. Leave out some of the lexical words (the words carrying information) and challenge a friend to work out what they might be.

> **Key point –** We often work out what kind of text we are reading by the style of sentences it contains.

COPYMASTER 3A–F

NEXT STEP

Sentence essentials 1: The subject

13

4 Sentence essentials 1: The subject

A ODD STORY

The following story does not make sense. Can you explain why not?

> Sat down on the doorstep. Wouldn't move. Just sat there. Then got up and ran down the path. Got to the gate. Jumped over it. Ran up to the milkman and jumped on him.

You probably worked out who the story was about by the end. But what made it difficult to follow? In one sentence, try to explain what was odd about the story.

B GUESS THE SUBJECT

Almost all sentences in English need a **subject**. This is the person or animal or thing that sentences are about.

In the short story in activity A the subject is a dog. See if you can work out who or what the subject is in the five sentences below. For each one, write down the subject (from column A, B or C) that fits best, followed by the rest of the sentence.

A: HUMAN	B: ANIMAL	C: THING
LAURA	MY HAMSTER	THE VAN
BILAL	A VULTURE	A GO-CART
AUNTIE MAVIS	TIDDLES THE	MUM'S CAR
MY FRIEND	GOLDFISH	

1. _____ was away from school today because she was ill.
2. _____ tried to swim away when it saw my shadow.
3. _____ was parked at the side of the road.
4. For breakfast _____ ate toast.
5. _____ sat on the chimneypot watching people.

Now look at the sentences you have written. If the subject was taken from the 'human' box, write A at the end of the sentence. Would any other subject have fitted from box B or C? If so, write those letters down as well.

14

C | CONTINUE THE SUBJECT

In the next exercise, you have the subjects but not what they actually did. Think up some ideas for what the subjects might have done. Then, in brackets at the end, write down whether each subject is human (A), animal (B) or a thing (C). Here is an example that is done for you:

★ The hedgehog ...   lay on the ground in a heap. (B)

  or   drank a saucer of milk. (B)

  or   had a terrible toothache. (B)

Notice that you can add lots of detail to the subject of a sentence – like this:

★ <u>The woman</u> telephoned the police.

★ <u>The angry woman</u> rang the police.

★ <u>The angry and breathless woman</u> rang the police.

★ <u>The woman who was completely out of breath</u> rang the police.

Make your examples as lively as possible.

1 The planet ...

2 The large snake ...

3 The sandwich ...

4 The burglar ...

5 The coffee-machine ...

Remember to write in sentences, so that the reader can follow your ideas. Don't forget the capital letter at the beginning and full stop at the end.

Follow-on : Take any five subjects from those listed in activity B. Use them as the subjects of new sentences, this time adding more detail to each one.

> **Key point –** Sentences need subjects: the person, animal or thing that is the 'star' of the sentence. It is usually in the first half of a sentence.

COPYMASTER  **Changing the subject**

15

5 Changing the subject

Learning objective:
to look at the way you can use pronouns to avoid repeating the subject too much

A   BORING BITS

In the last unit you saw that every sentence has a subject – the person, animal or thing that does something. Look at what happens if the writer keeps repeating the same subject in a paragraph:

Helicopters

Helicopters date back 250 years. The first helicopter was invented in Russia in 1754. The first helicopter was a spring-driven model. Helicopters became most popular in the 1930s, though in those days helicopters could not rise much above the ground. Helicopters can easily spin out of control. Early helicopters would begin to spin round while their propellers stayed in the same place.

Perhaps you find the subject matter of this paragraph quite entertaining. But no one would find the written style interesting. Why not? How could the writer make the paragraph more interesting to read?

16

B ADDING PRONOUNS

Pronouns allow us to keep the same subject going without always repeating the same word.

Pronouns are words like these:

it   she   he   they   us   we   me   him   her   you   I

Rewrite the helicopter paragraph. Use 'it' or 'they' to avoid repeating the subject word too often.

Follow-on: Write a paragraph on one of the following topics *without* using pronouns. Instead, just keep repeating the topic word. Then give the paragraph to a friend and ask her to improve it by changing some of the nouns to pronouns.

Choose a topic:

★ school dinners

★ computers

★ a favourite television programme.

Beware of using too many pronouns – you could leave your reader confused. Experiment with changing subjects to pronouns and see what the effect is.

> **Key point –** Pronouns are important words in helping you to avoid repeating the subject too much. They can make texts more interesting and varied to read.

Sentence essentials 2: Verbs

6 Sentence essentials 2: Verbs

Learning objective:
to understand what verbs are and how they give
sentences their power

A SPOTTING VERBS

Working on your own or with a partner, read these sentences. They are all
about fingers. You will find that they all feel 'odd' because there is a word
missing where the ✳ is. See if you can think of words that might fit in the gaps.

1. The nail on your thumb ✳ faster than the nail on your little finger.
2. The longest ever fingernail ✳ 64.7 cm long.
3. Fingerprint tests ✳ first ✳ in Britain in 1948.
4. Some giant pandas ✳ ✳ with up to 14 extra fingers.
5. Fingernails stop ✳ after you ✳.

The later sentences are more difficult to follow because they have more words
missing. Write down some of the words that might fit in each sentence.
There may be more than one answer. Use a table like the one on the left.

SENTENCE	MISSING WORD(S)
1	
2	
3	
4	
5	

Now look at the words in your list. What have they got in common?
The answer is that they all tell us about something happening.
You might know them as <u>doing words</u>.

★ Some 'doing words' tell you when something happens:

   was, are, is, have

★ Some tell you what happens: eating, think, moves

In grammar, all doing words are called **verbs**.

B TROUBLE AT THE SEASIDE

Verbs are probably the most important words we use in sentences. Without
them we wouldn't know what was going on. Look at the newspaper story on
the next page, which has no verbs. See if you can guess what the missing
words are.

With a friend, compare the possible words you could use in each space.

LOCAL MAN * INTO THE SEA!

A local man yesterday * 3 metres into the harbour. Lifeguards * * when tourists suddenly * cries for help * from the water. They * to the nearest telephone to * for assistance.

C | **CHANGING VERBS**

Look again at that headline:

LOCAL MAN * INTO THE SEA!

These are what a group of Year 8 students thought of as the missing word (including some crazy ones!):

falls drops jumps swims breathes walks parachutes spits cooks

Would all of these verbs make sense in the sentence? Which would and which would not? Try to explain why.

Follow-on : Write your own newspaper story with the verbs in each sentence missing. Aim to write 50–100 words. If you can't think of a topic, imagine a fire being discovered in a local shop. Then challenge a friend to work out what the missing verbs are.

> **Key point –** Verbs tell us what is happening in a sentence or what someone is doing (for example 'jump'). Verbs also tell us <u>when</u> something happens – in the present, past or future (<u>is</u> jumping, <u>has</u> jumped, <u>will</u> jump).

COPYMASTER 6 A/B   **Simple sentences**

7 Simple sentences

A SIMPLE STARTERS

The following text has a capital letter at the beginning. It has a full stop at the end. But it needs another punctuation mark in the middle to make its meaning clearer. If you were writing the text, what would you use – a full stop or a comma?

★ The old man walked down the street he looked tired.

Which punctuation marks would you use in the middle of these next sentences to make them clearer for the reader?

1. The dog looked fierce I kept well back.
2. The child on the bike was riding quickly it was a smart machine.
3. Mrs Andrews shouted hello she knows me well.

B SHORTIES

Sometimes it can feel odd to write very short sentences. Look at what one Year 8 student, Lisa, says:

> In my work I can sometimes feel that there's a break in the sentences. I know that it needs some kind of punctuation mark. Often a full stop feels 'too strong' so I put in a comma and hope it's right!

This is how many students feel, and as a result they can end up with lots of corrections on their written work.

Remember that a sentence usually has these basic ingredients:

★ **a subject** + **a verb**

This means that sentences can be very short – like these examples below:

★ I enjoy silence.

★ I sit still.

★ I think.

All of these have a subject (I) and a verb (enjoy, sit, think). They are called simple sentences – not because they are short but because they contain one subject and one verb. A larger simple sentence might read:

★ The old grey and white cat finally moved.

It has one subject (the old grey and white cat) and one verb (moved).

Look at the text below. Copy it out by adding punctuation marks to it. Decide whether you need to use full stops or commas. The important thing is – do not guess. If it is a complete sentence with subject and verb, show that it is complete by using a full stop.

Sad dog story!
The dog was looking unhappy he sat on the floor he looked up at his owner she ignored him and carried on with her paperwork the dog sniffed hoping the owner would pay a bit more attention to him she didn't he finally got up and left the room he went to the stairs and sulked

Follow-on: What happens next in this sad dog story? Write the next paragraph, without using any punctuation. But as you write, try to vary the length of sentences you are writing. Then give the paragraph to a friend, who should try to mark the sentence boundaries correctly.

> **Key point –** Short sentences are fine! Use full stops, not commas, to show the end of each sentence, even if it is very short.

8 Simple sentences in context

Learning objective:
to look at how simple sentences can add variety to your written style

A RAMBLERS' ASSOCIATION

Look at this spoken text from Sam, aged three and a half:

> I went to the zoo and it was very big and I saw an elephant and his name was George and there were penguins and I had peanut butter sandwiches and my mummy said look at that big monkey Sam and it was nice ...

As we learn to speak, we all go through that phase of stringing sentences together with 'and'. But it can get very repetitive and difficult to follow. Using simple sentences at the start and end of your paragraphs can make your work feel much more interesting. Here's an extract from Toni's book review:

> I usually like J D Fannon's books.(1) This one was different.(2) It began in the usual way with a really entertaining opening and all the main characters were introduced.(3) Then it seemed to lose the thread a bit and the way it showed the women characters actually made me feel quite uncomfortable.(4) I carried on reading it to the end but I wouldn't recommend it to anyone.(5) It was too sexist.(6)

Try putting 'but' between sentences 1 and 2, and put 'because' between sentences 5 and 6 and notice how the text feels different. Then read Toni's original text again. See how a simple sentence or two at the start leads the reader in. Then the simple sentence at the end gives a strong final effect.

B FACT PACK

Now you try it. Take the list of facts given on the page opposite and use it to write a paragraph which starts and ends with short, simple sentences. You don't have to use all the facts, and you can change the order of the information. But try to come up with a paragraph which is interesting – in its content and its feel.

Locust Fact Pack

★ The largest plague of locusts ever: California 1949.

★ Covered 3,000 square miles.

★ Swarm probably contained 4,000 million locusts.

★ Weighed 800 thousand tonnes.

★ Male locusts rub their legs together to make noise.

★ Can be heard up to a quarter of a mile away.

★ Some people eat locusts.

★ Recipes: baked locusts with honey, locust cake, roast locust with pepper.

★ No one is really sure why they swarm.

Notice that because these are notes, they don't always contain a sentence (for example: 'Weighed 800 thousand tonnes.')

Follow-on: Compare your fact-pack text with a friend's.

Key point – Simple sentences at the start and end of paragraphs can make your writing more interesting to read.

Compound sentences

9 Compound sentences

Learning objective:
to learn what compound sentences are

A COMPOUNDS

In science a compound is a substance made up of other substances. In English, a compound sentence is made up of a number of **clauses** joined together by linking words (**conjunctions**). For example, look at this long sentence:

★ I liked the football match <u>and</u> I enjoyed the table tennis <u>but</u> I wasn't keen on the wrestling.

It contains three clauses:

★ I liked the football match
★ I enjoyed the table tennis
★ I wasn't keen on the wrestling

and two linking words:

★ and
★ but

Clauses are units of meaning built around a verb. They tell you who or what did something and what they did. They are parts of whole sentences.

Look at the five sentences below. See if you can work out how many clauses each one has. Then write down the linking words you spot. Use a table like the one on the left. The first example is done for you.

NUMBER OF CLAUSES	LINKING WORDS (CONJUNCTIONS)
1 2	and
2	
3	
4	
5	

1. Mrs Jones walked into the room and we all went quiet.
2. The homework was difficult but I finished it all.
3. The room was dark but I walked in and soon felt fine.
4. The supermarket was closed but I knew another one and we went to that one instead.
5. I got up and went downstairs but suddenly I remembered I had no milk for my cornflakes and so I went back upstairs and got dressed and went down stairs again and went out to buy some milk and I got to the shop and it was shut.

B MAKING LINKS

The most common conjunctions in compound sentences are:

★ and　　　　but　　　　or

Here is a heap of clauses. Use the conjunctions to link them together. See if you can tell a short story in just two or three compound sentences.

★ I waited at the bus stop
★ there was no one there
★ there was no sign of a bus
★ it was very quiet
★ I decided to walk
★ it was getting dark
★ the leaves of the tree began to rustle
★ was it the sound of footsteps?
★ I decided not to walk
★ I went back to the bus stop
★ a bus turned up

Follow-on: Compare your short story with those of others in your class.

> **Key point –** Compound sentences are clauses linked by the conjunctions <u>and</u>, <u>but</u> and <u>or</u>.

10 Compound sentences in context

Learning objective:
to look at how you could use compound sentences
in your own writing

A SOUND EFFECTS

If a paragraph has too many short, simple sentences it can feel very broken-up or disjointed:

★ The box was full. It contained lots of books. It was very heavy. I couldn't carry it alone. I asked for help. Everyone laughed.

If a paragraph has one or two very long compound sentences, it can feel confusing and uncontrolled:

★ The box was full and it contained lots of books and was very heavy and I couldn't carry it alone but I asked for help and everyone laughed.

The more you write, the more confident you become in knowing when to use a compound sentence and when to stick to a simple sentence. Work as the editor on the following text. At present it has no punctuation and no conjunctions. Rewrite it using:

★ some simple sentences (ending with a full stop)
★ some compound sentences (clauses linked by and, but, or).

Unhappy Memory
I don't really like dogs it all goes back to my childhood I can't remember exactly how old I was I was lying on the floor I was just watching television 'Thunderbirds' was on it was my favourite programme my Uncle Jim arrived he brought his huge black Labrador dog with him it might have been a sheepdog I hadn't noticed them come into the room next thing that I knew Texan was standing over me pinning me to the floor I couldn't move I was too terrified I simply lay there last thing that I remember was watching Thunderbird Two take off through a face full of tears

B | MEMORY MODULE

Choose one of the subjects below and write your own paragraph based on a memory. Use it to practise writing a variety of sentences – simple and compound.

★ the first thing you remember happening

★ a friend you no longer have

★ an embarrassing moment

★ a special pet

Follow-on : Redraft your paragraph. Experiment with changing the structure of it, adding another simple sentence to the start, middle or end, or changing simple sentences into compounds by adding conjunctions. Be critical of what you have written – keep trying to improve the style.

> **Key point –** Like simple sentences, compound sentences shouldn't be used all the time. Used with other sentence types they can add variety to your writing.

Complex sentences 1:
Relative clauses

Complex sentences 1: Wh- clauses

Learning objective:
to learn about the first type of complex sentences –
using Wh- clauses

Complex sentences give your writing style the most variety and flexibility of all.

There are three types of complex sentence. This unit looks at the first type.

A | WH- CLAUSES

Look at this sentence:

★ The dog, <u>which was beginning to look unhappy</u>, ran away.

This starts as a simple sentence: The dog ran away. The wh- clause in the middle allows the writer to give more detail about the dog. Notice that your wh- clause can start with <u>which</u>, <u>who</u> or <u>that</u>, depending on what the subject is.

Use the five cartoons below to write five sentences, each containing a wh- clause. The first example is done for you.

1. My cheesecake, which is stale, tastes horrible.
2. ....
3. ....
4. ....
5. ....

Now look at the simple sentences in the table below and, where the arrow points, add a wh- clause. Try to make them as crazy as possible.

Style hint: When we use wh- clauses, we sometimes place commas around them if this makes the meaning clearer. These are called parenthetical commas – they work like brackets (parentheses).

SUBJECT	▼	REST OF SENTENCE
1 THE FOOLISH SOLDIER,		, TRIPPED UP.
2 MY GREAT UNCLE VERNON,		, IS A MILLIONAIRE.
3 THAT LARGE GLASS OF COLA,		, HAS PROBABLY GONE FLAT.
4 THIS NEW ALBUM,		, SOUNDS AWFUL.
5 YOUR COMPUTER,		, HAS JUST MADE AN ODD BLEEPING SOUND.

Follow-on : Think of five more sentences which have wh-clauses. You might link them all to one topic – for example, a bad journey to school, or swimming underwater.

> **Key point** – Wh- clauses are one way of adding detail to sentences. We sometimes use parenthetical commas (pairs of commas) to make our meaning clearer to the reader.

COPYMASTER 11 A/B

Complex sentences 2: -ing clauses

12 Complex sentences 2: -ing clauses

Learning objective:
to learn about the second type of complex sentence :
-ing clauses

A -ING CLAUSES

This is the second type of complex sentence.

-ing-clause sentences have two parts. One part of them, as in almost all sentences, contains the subject. The other part has an 'ing' verb. Here's an example:

★ Waiting at the bus stop, I noticed a ten-pound note.

(subject: 'I' – that's the person who is doing the waiting and who notices the money.)

Usually, the verb is placed before the subject. Look what happens if you switch the order:

★ I noticed a ten-pound note, waiting at the bus stop.

Can you see the problem here? It sounds as if it is the ten-pound note that is waiting at the bus stop.

Here are the first halves of some -ing clauses. You make up the second halves. You are given the subject of the main clause – try to finish the sentence off with your own ideas.

1 Sitting on the cushion, the cat ...
2 Finishing her ice cream, Mavis ...
3 Deciding it was getting late, I ...
4 Hoping it wouldn't rain, Mrs Priestland ...
5 Jumping up onto the truck, Old Sam ...

B YOUR TURN

This time you think up 5–10 -ing-clause sentences. Use the verbs below if you want to, or choose your own.

★ thinking   wondering   diving   sailing   kicking   washing   gliding
  failing   straining   printing   clicking   opening

C | DANGLING DANGER!

Sometimes our sentences become silly if the -ing clause is left dangling, so that it doesn't really fit with the main clause. Look at these three examples where the -ing clause is left dangling. Can you see why they don't quite make sense?

★ Sitting on top of the hill, it started to rain.
★ Walking down the road, the bus zoomed past.
★ Eating my ice cream, it fell on the floor.

For the following sentences say whether the -ing clause is a dangler (D) or makes sense (S).

1. Sitting by the lake, the fish were surfacing.
2. Watching all the clouds, I became dizzy.
3. Thinking of the holidays, the teacher grew dreamy.
4. Finishing his first course, the pudding looked great.
5. Swilling out the sink, the dirt hardly moved.

Follow-on: Write a paragraph about one of the topics below. Try to use a variety of sentence types: simple, compound and complex.

Possible topics:

★ the opening of a science fiction story
★ a description of the journey you make each day from school to home.

> **Key point –** -ing clauses are another way of adding variety to your writing – but you have to watch that you don't leave them dangling.

13 Complex sentences 3: Adverbial kick-starter:

Learning objective:
to learn about the third type of complex sentences – adverbial kick-starters

A ADVERBIAL KICK-STARTERS

'Adverbial clauses' is the term for a group of words which can be used in complex sentences. Like -ing-clause sentences, they work in two parts.

The following are some examples:

★ <u>Although</u> <u>I could hardly see</u>, I managed to find the light switch.

★ <u>Whenever</u> <u>I travel by boat</u>, I feel sick.

★ <u>However</u> <u>hard I work</u>, he always thinks I'm messing around.

★ <u>Despite</u> <u>taking all your advice</u>, I still got it wrong.

Below are the adverbial phrases and subjects of eight sentences. You fill the gaps to make interesting, lively sentences.

ADVERBIAL CLAUSE		SUBJECT
1 ALTHOUGH ...	,	MRS TAYLOR ...
2 AFTER ...	,	THE CAT ...
3 ALTHOUGH ...	,	MY BEST FRIEND ...
4 BECAUSE ...	,	YOU ...
5 DESPITE ...	,	THE DOLPHIN ...
6 WHENEVER ...	,	I ...
7 WHOEVER ...	,	SHE ...
8 WHEREVER ...	,	THEY ...

B ADVERBIAL FINISHERS

'Adverbial clauses' do not have to be at the start of sentences. Try completing these examples:

1 I hate cheese, though _____ .

2 She won't be in later, because _____ .

3 I still don't understand this, despite _____ .

Follow-on: Adverbial kick-starters are especially useful in more formal writing. But use them too much and they become repetitive, as this postcard from Dan in Majorca shows.

Although I enjoyed the holiday, the weather was disappointing. Despite packing all my summer stuff, I couldn't use all of it. Whenever I decided to have a day on the beach, it always seemed to rain. Because I hated the weather I stayed indoors quite a lot. After a long time spent lounging about in the hotel it became quite boring.

Dan needs to vary his style more. Rewrite his postcard so that it feels more 'natural' and less formal.

> **Key point –** Adverbial kick-starters are two-part sentences. They can create a formal feel in writing. As with other sentence styles, they should be varied.

14 Sentence variety

Learning objective:
to explore the way different types of sentences can make your writing more effective

A   SENTENCE LENGTH

How long do you think the average written sentence in English is?

(a) 9 words
(b) 17 words
(c) 24 words
(d) 37 words

After you have thought about it, look at the bottom of the next page for the answer.

Imagine what writing would be like if sentences were always about the same length. Read the passages below and choose the word you think best describes the effect.

> ### Style A – lots of short, simple sentences
>
> It was cold. I was hungry. I ate quickly. I went out. I walked. I still felt cold. I jumped a little. I ran around. I clapped my hands together. I blew on my fingers. I went home again.

1 Which word best describes the effect of Style A: interesting, dull, menacing, tense, disturbing, repetitive, unexciting, slow-moving, nerve-racking, tedious, descriptive?

2 Test what happens when you add the conjunctions 'and', 'but' and 'or' to make some of the simple sentences into compound sentences.

> ### Style B – lots of fairly long, compound sentences
>
> The old woman walked into the newsagent's and asked for a bag of Jelly Babies and the newsagent got some from a jar and gave them to the old woman. She said 'thank you' and left the shop and walked round the corner to a bench and sat down and opened the bag and ate the Jelly Babies. Then she put the bag in the bin and walked away.

34

3 Which word best describes the effect of Style B: interesting, dull, menacing, tense, disturbing, repetitive, unexciting, slow-moving, nerve-racking, tedious, descriptive?

4 Test what happens when you take out some of the conjunctions to make some simple sentences.

Style C – lots of complex sentences

When the boat had left, we sat at the side of the harbour and waited. Despite the awful weather, someone was supposed to collect us. Feeling colder, we looked for shelter. We saw a figure walking towards us through the fog, after we had waited quite a while. Slowly becoming more visible, she approached us. When she reached us she apologised for being late. Pleased that we had been met, which was our main worry, we followed her to the car.

5 Which word best describes the effect of Style C: interesting, dull, menacing, tense, disturbing, repetitive, unexciting, slow-moving, nerve-racking, tedious, descriptive?

6 Test what happens when you vary some of the sentences by changing them to simple or compound sentences, or by changing the clauses round within a sentence. (Look at sentence 2 – try reversing the order of the two clauses.)

7 Niam in Year 9 says: 'This isn't really a fair test of sentences. The last paragraph is more interesting than the others. It is about a more interesting subject. So that's why the last one seems better than the others.' Do you agree?

> **Key point –** The best writing usually entertains or informs or amuses us. This is not just because of what it is about. It is also a result of a varied sentence style – a mix of simple, compound and complex sentences.

(The average written sentence in English is 17 words long.)

COPYMASTER 14 A–C

Self-assessment page: Sentences

Use this page to track your progress. Find out where your strengths and weaknesses are. If there are parts of the 'Sentences' section which you could not understand fully, use the Homework File as further practice.

Use the Progress Chart to note your score.

1 The subject is an essential ingredient in most sentences. Which of these examples does NOT contain a subject?

    a) I love chocolates.
    b) The old dog lay on the carpet.
    c) Sit down over there.
    d) Can I have a piece of cake, please?

2 Verbs are also important in most sentences. Which of these sentences does NOT contain a verb?

    a) The computer exploded loudly.
    b) My bike needs mending.
    c) The newsagent's shop at the back of the estate.
    d) The firework made a strange fizzing noise.

3 Here are four types of sentence. Label each one using the appropriate letter (S = statement; Q = question; C = command; E = exclamation).

    a) Are you going to work today?
    b) This cake seems to have something nasty in it.
    c) What an amazing concert!
    d) Open that door quickly.

4 Look at these three sentence styles. Which is simple (S); which is compound (C); and which is complex (Co)?

    a) I enjoyed the film and would like to see it again.
    b) The party at Sarah's house was excellent.
    c) The sports centre, which only opened last year, looks amazing.

Use your score to show you any areas you need to revise. Then move on to 'Section 2: Clauses and phrases'.

Clauses and phrases:
Creating islands of words

AIMS:

★ to look at the way sentences can be made up of 'islands of words'

★ to help you to use clauses and phrases in your own writing

In this section you will learn:

★ to identify clauses

★ more about the different types of clauses

★ that these clauses create different effects in your writing – often giving 'main' and 'background' information

★ to spot phrases and look at their function in clauses.

Remember:

★ the Homework File has activity sheets so that you can practise all the skills you learn

★ there is a self-assessment test at the end of the section, so that you can chart your progress.

16 Understanding clauses

Learning objective:
to understand what clauses are and to see the effect they have on the sentences we write

A   CLAUSE-SPOTTING

A clause is a group of words built around a verb.

Here are some examples (with the verb underlined):

★ <u>sitting</u> on the bus

★ he <u>ate</u> his sandwich

★ <u>thinking</u> about the money

Clauses form parts of sentences. In a *simple* sentence there will be just one clause:

★ <u>I hate eating catfood</u>.

In a *compound* sentence there will be more than one clause. Each clause will be connected by a conjunction. For example, this sentence contains three clauses joined together by two conjunctions:

★ <u>I hate eating cat food</u> and <u>I'm not fond of dog food</u> but <u>I quite fancy that bowl of milk</u>.

In a complex sentence there might be several clauses:

★ <u>Eating slowly</u>, <u>the old man scratched his chin</u>. (= 2 clauses)

★ <u>The old man sitting in the chair</u>, <u>who was fond of cheese</u>, <u>scratched his chin</u>. (= 3 clauses)

Look at the following sentences and, for each one, write down how many clauses you think there are.

1. The shopkeeper wiped the window.
2. She looked outside.
3. It was getting dark and the streetlights were coming on.
4. She was bored and looked up at the clock.
5. Ticking quietly, the clock said 5.24.
6. Then the shop bell rang loudly as another customer arrived and asked for some help.

B CLAUSE TYPES

Clauses are useful in sentences because they allow us to give more than one piece of information at a time. Look carefully at these sentences and you will see that one clause carries the main message of the sentence. It is the *main* clause. The other clause gives background information.

Example

★ Sitting at the table, the child began to weep.

The main clause is 'the child began to weep'. The other clause gives extra detail (background information), about where the child was sitting. We call it the *subordinate* clause.

★ The cow, which had spent the day in the sun, was brought into the barn.

Main clause = 'The cow was brought into the barn';
Subordinate clause = 'which had spent the day in the sun'.

Look at the following sentences and decide which is the main clause (M) and which is the subordinate clause (S).

1 Thinking back (A), the man regretted his actions (B).
2 Sitting there (A), placing his head in his hands (B), he felt worried (C).
3 He thought hard (A) about what he had done (B).
4 His face, which was pale and tense (A), shone with beads of sweat (B).
5 He got up (A), wishing he had not said those final words (B).

> **Key point** – Clauses are units of meaning built around a verb. They add detail to sentences by allowing you to show more than one thing happening within a sentence. There are two types of clauses – main and subordinate.

17 Understanding phrases

A PHRASE-SPOTTING

We often use groups of words that go together well but which do not stand alone as sentences.

Look at these phrases:

★ my hamster
★ on the bus
★ out of time
★ behind the scenes
★ over the hill

What makes them phrases rather than sentences? It is chiefly the fact that they don't make sense on their own. For example:

★ On the bus

This does not make sense because it does not have a subject – <u>who</u> is on the bus? It also does not have a verb – what are they <u>doing</u> on the bus?

So a sentence containing this phrase might read:

★ Sally was sitting quietly <u>on the bus</u>.

Take these phrases and put them into separate sentences. If you want, you can try to write them as a paragraph, so that one sentence follows another. But be warned: that will prove very difficult.

1 over the moon
2 the fat pony
3 my new computer-game
4 through the tunnel
5 a cup of tea
6 underneath the street lamp
7 on television
8 am laughing

B | PHRASES IN ACTION

Phrases are useful for giving short pieces of information. In speech we often use them to answer questions:

Where's the nearest newsagent's?   <u>Round the corner.</u>

What's that you're holding?   <u>My new personal stereo.</u>

Where did you get that scar?   <u>In a fight.</u>

See how snappy these answers are – they give just the essential information. But in writing, we are often expected to use full sentences – especially in assessed conditions.

How would you convert the following phrase answers in a reading test into sentences?

1. Why did the woman leave the room?   <u>Too stuffy.</u>
2. Where did she go?   <u>Into the car-park.</u>
3. Who did she see there?   <u>The old man with the funny walk.</u>
4. What did she do?   <u>Went towards him.</u>
5. Where did they go?   <u>Home.</u>

> **Key point –** Phrases are groups of words which carry meaning, but they cannot usually stand alone in writing or in speech, except as short answers to questions. It can be useful to think of phrases as 'islands of words' within sentences.

COPYMASTER

Self-assessment page: Clauses and phrases

1 Both clauses and phrases are examples of 'islands of words'. What does a clause usually contain that a phrase does not?

Look at the following sentence, which is made up of two clauses:

★ I saw the wild dog again (A), while I was sitting on the swing (B).

2 Which is the main clause (main event)?

3 Which is the subordinate clause (background event)?

4 Look at the following sentence. Write down an example of a phrase it contains:

★ I waited at the back of the house.

Remember that many people find clauses and phrases baffling. But stick with it. Use the Homework File to gain more practice, and perhaps return to the topic after you have looked at the next section – 'Word classes'.

Word classes:
Using language more precisely

AIMS:

★ to look at the way different types of words work in sentences

★ to help you make your writing more lively and precise

In this section you will:

★ explore how we change the shape of words to give information about what we mean (inflection)

★ look at the way different types of nouns carry important information

★ look at how verbs can give 'muscle' to our sentences

★ experiment with ways of showing <u>when</u> something happened (tenses)

★ explore descriptive tools – adjectives and adverbs

★ learn more about other word classes.

Remember:

★ the Homework File has activity sheets so that you can practise all the skills you learn

★ there is a self-assessment test at the end of the section, so that you can chart your progress.

19 Word structure

A WORD STRUCTURES

We take words for granted. From around the age of one we begin to use them, one by one. Suddenly we start to learn more and more very quickly. Then we go mad, wanting to have words to describe everything we see and think about. A child of two can use around 250 words. A child of seven probably knows more than 5 000.

Because we take words for granted, it is easy to forget that they have their own patterns and structures. For example, look at these words and answer the questions.

1 Word: <u>cats</u>

How many cats are there – one or more?

2 Word: <u>dogs</u>

How many dogs are there – one or more?

3 Word: <u>fish</u>

How many fish are there – one or more?

4 Which of these questions was most tricky to answer?

Try to say why.

B WORD PATTERNS

Activity A is useful in reminding you how we use words to gain information. Without thinking about it, we add bits to the end of words to tell us:

★ how many things there are (singular or plural)

★ what something is like (for example: big ➤ bigger ➤ biggest).

Changing words in this way is called **inflection**. The units we add to the ends of words are **suffixes**.

Look at the list of words and suffixes below. Try to describe in a sentence how the suffix changes the meaning of the word. The first is done for you as an example.

Sometimes you will find it tricky to think of words to describe how the meaning has changed. If you want, you could instead write a sentence as an example to show what the word means.

	STEM	SUFFIX	DESCRIPTION
1	HOUSE	S	THE SUFFIX SHOWS THAT THERE IS MORE THAN ONE HOUSE.
2	NOISE	S	
3	SMALL	EST	
4	SMALL	ER	
5	ARRANGE	MENT	
6	QUICK	LY	
7	SAD	NESS	
8	THINK	ING	

Follow-on: We can also change the meanings of words by adding **prefixes** to the front of them. Look at the list of prefixes and suffixes below. Imagine you are explaining to an overseas student of English what each bit does. Try to explain each one as simply as possible, in a single sentence, giving an example to show what you mean.

	PREFIX		SUFFIX
1	PRE-	4	-ING
2	DIS-	5	-LY
3	EX-	6	-ED

Key point – The structure of words gives us important clues about meaning – especially how many people or things there are.

20 Nouns

Learning objective:
to learn more about nouns or 'naming words'

A NAMING NAMES

You might not be sure what **nouns** are. They are the words we use to name things, people and actions. They often carry the most important information in a sentence. Look at what happens if you leave the nouns out of a shopping list:

> 2 ✳ of ✳, a large ✳, 3 ✳ and a ✳ ✳ of ✳.

or out of a description of a science experiment:

> First we put some ✳ into a ✳. Then we lit the ✳. We added some ✳. We watched. Suddenly there was a bright ✳ and a loud ✳.

Using the word bank below, have a go at guessing which nouns might fit into the gaps.

ammonia tins test-tube family flame custard acid

lemon flash pack bang cornflakes apples

Were there any nouns here which could have been in <u>both</u> texts?

B NOUN FEATURES

Just by looking at most nouns you can tell whether there is one of them or more than one – whether they are **singular** or **plural**. Look at this table.

SINGULAR NOUNS	PLURAL NOUNS
DOG	DOGS
CHEESEBURGER	CHEESEBURGERS

Most nouns simply add 's' at the end to show whether they are singular or plural. Not all do. Look at these nouns in sentences. For each one, say whether you think the underlined noun is singular (s) or plural (p):

1. I noticed all the <u>sheep</u> in the field.
2. What badly behaved <u>children</u> they were.
3. I hope that <u>aircraft</u> lands safely.
4. He was nearly attacked by those <u>fish</u>.
5. She heard the <u>mice</u> in the attic.

Now look back at those five sentences. How did you work out whether the underlined noun was plural or singular? After all, there was no 's' at the end to help you. For each one, write down the main clue in the sentence that helped you to work out whether the noun was singular or plural.

Follow-on: Write a paragraph of text on one of the topics below and leave all the nouns out. Then create a word bank beneath the paragraph. Ask a friend to see if she can place the words from the word bank correctly into the text.

Topics:

★ Describe a journey you have been on – for example, to school.

★ Write a recipe you know well.

★ Describe your kitchen.

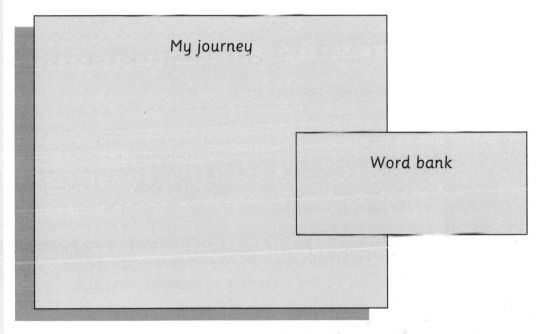

My journey

Word bank

Key point – Nouns are vital in sentences. They carry important information. Nouns are either singular (one) or plural (more than one).

Noun types

21 Noun types

A THREE NOUN TYPES

You need to know three types of nouns:

★ concrete

★ abstract

★ proper

A <u>concrete</u> noun is something that you can see or touch – for example, a computer, a scarf, a bus, or a pineapple.

An <u>abstract</u> noun is an idea or emotion, something you can't really see or touch – for example, happiness, anger, the future, heaven, fitness.

A <u>proper</u> noun is the name of a person, place or even time. It usually begins with a capital letter – for example, Sara, India, Christmas.

This paragraph contains plenty of nouns. For each one, work out whether it is concrete (C), abstract (A) or proper (P). Be warned – it can sometimes be hard to decide.

> <u>Mrs Wallace</u> (1) set out on <u>foot</u> (2) to visit her old <u>friend</u> (3), <u>Mandy</u> (4). The <u>night</u> (5) was dark and the <u>air</u> (6) was cold. But it was <u>winter</u> (7) so this was the <u>weather</u> (8) you would expect. As she walked the wet <u>pavement</u> (9), Mrs Wallace noticed <u>something</u> (10) that created a <u>feeling</u> (11) of <u>terror</u> (12) in her <u>heart</u> (13). She lifted her <u>eyes</u> (14) quickly upwards, and came face to <u>face</u> (15) with <u>hatred</u> (16).

B NOUNS IN TEXTS

You now know that there are three main types of nouns. The type we use depends on the context we are in. Have a look at the list of contexts on the right, and decide which type of noun we would be most likely to use. See if you can explain why.

48

CONTEXT	TYPE OF NOUN CONCRETE, ABSTRACT OR PROPER? (C) (A) (P)	WHY?
1 PICKING PEOPLE FOR A FOOTBALL TEAM		
2 A SHOPPING LIST		
3 A POEM ABOUT SADNESS		
4 A GUIDE TO KEEPING FISH		
5 A BIOGRAPHY OF A FAMOUS PERSON		
6 INSTRUCTIONS FOR HOW TO GET ACROSS TOWN		
7 A GHOST STORY		

(A fourth type of noun is called the <u>collective</u> noun. It is a less important type, used to describe groups that things belong to – for example, a <u>pack</u> of lions, a <u>flock</u> of seagulls. You can find out more about this in the Homework File.)

Follow-on : Look back at the story about Mrs Wallace. Continue it for two or three more paragraphs, underlining the nouns you use.

> **Key point –** There are three main types of nouns. We use a variety of types according to the context in which we are writing or speaking.

COPYMASTER 21 A–D   **Verbs**

49

22 Verbs

A VERB POWER

You already know from section 1 that verbs are an essential ingredient of most sentences (see unit 6). Now you can learn more about different types of verbs.

Ask most students what a verb is and they will say 'a doing word'. Often that's true. Look at the cartoons below. Each one shows the subject of a sentence – a person, animal or thing that is doing something.
For each one decide what the subject is **doing** – what the verb is that describes the subject's action.

Write down six verbs, one for each cartoon.

50

B | DYNAMIC OR STATIVE VERBS

Now look back at your six verbs. Is it accurate to describe them all as 'doing' words? Look at the list below. These are all verbs but some of them don't seem to involve doing.

★ eating   dreaming   hoping   windsurfing   throwing

Three of these words involve doing. They are called **dynamic** verbs. The other two are not really active. They are called **stative** verbs. They often describe states of mind – for example, thoughts and feelings.

From the list of five verbs:

1 Which are the three dynamic verbs?

2 Which are the two stative verbs?

Follow-on : Now think of six sentences of your own. Three of them should contain dynamic verbs. Three of them should contain stative verbs. As the subject for your sentences you might choose:

★ someone who has a day off work and is planning what to do.

> **Key point** – There are two main categories of verbs – dynamic (doing) and stative (often describing feelings and thoughts).

Learning objective:
to look at the effect dynamic and stative verbs can have in texts

A THE TERRIFYING CYCLOPS

Some verbs are dynamic (run, hit, attack, eat, sing) and others are stative, describing emotions and feelings. A frequently-used stative verb is **be** (was, am, are, is, will be ...). This verb is very useful for describing things and people, and for giving information. Look at how it works in the texts below.

The Cyclops was a horrifying one-eyed monster in Greek myth. Here are some paragraphs by writer Anthony Horowitz. In one extract, he uses mostly stative verbs. In the other, he uses a few more dynamic verbs. Read both extracts through and use a table like the one opposite to spot some of the different verbs.

The Eye of the Cyclops

The Cyclops <u>was</u> certainly a terrifying creature. It <u>was</u> about the height of a two-storey house with thick, curly hair, a matted (and usually filthy) beard and only one eye set square in the middle of its forehead. It <u>was</u> grotesquely ugly, extremely bad-tempered, inordinately violent and generally worth going a long way <u>to avoid</u>. All this, any good book of Greek myths will <u>tell</u> you. But what <u>is</u> less often <u>mentioned</u> <u>is</u> the fact that the Cyclops <u>was</u> also incredibly stupid. It <u>was</u> probably one of the most stupid monsters that every <u>lived</u>.

One day, <u>returning</u> to his cave after a hard day's work in the hills, he <u>was</u> astonished to find that he had <u>had</u> visitors. They <u>were</u> still there in fact, <u>sitting</u> in front of his fire and <u>feasting</u> on one of his sheep. There were about a dozen of them and, <u>looking</u> more closely, he <u>was</u> delighted to see that they <u>were</u> human beings.
Polyphemus <u>loved</u> human beings in his own way ... which was cooked or raw. What he particularly <u>liked</u> about them was the way their bones <u>crunched</u> between his teeth but never <u>got caught</u> in his throat.
The giant's face <u>lit up</u> in a great smile. It <u>was</u> also a horrible smile for, having just one eye in the middle of his forehead, everything he <u>did</u> with his face <u>was</u> rather horrible.

1 Which text uses more dynamic verbs?

2 Which text uses more stative verbs?

3 Write down two dynamic verbs and two stative verbs that the writer uses in each text.

PARAGRAPH A	PARAGRAPH B
ACTIVE	ACTIVE
1	1
2	2
STATIVE	STATIVE
1	1
2	2

Follow-on : Choose which extract (A or B) best fits each of the questions below. Write N if you're not sure and A+B if you think the best answer is both.

★ Which one grabs your attention more?

★ Which one has more happening?

★ Which one sets the scene better?

★ Which one tells you more about the Cyclops?

★ Which one feels more like an adventure story?

★ Which one feels more like a reference book on myths and legends?

> **Key point –** Dynamic and stative verbs can create powerfully different effects in texts.

24 Tenses

Learning objective:
to look at the way we use verbs to tell people when things take place

A | PAST, PRESENT AND FUTURE

When you listen to someone talking, how do you know whether they are talking about the past, the present or the future? One way is to listen out for certain words they use – **adverbs** and **adverbial phrases** which can say something about the time – such as <u>soon, yesterday, tomorrow, last week, next time, later,</u> and so on.

Read these sentences and work out which are the adverbs or adverbial phrases. The first one is done for you.

1. I'll see you <u>tomorrow</u> then.
2. Thanks for the money you gave me yesterday.
3. I hope to be back soon.
4. See you later.
5. It's still raining.
6. I found this at home last year.

There is more about adverbs later in this section.

B | VERB TENSES

Look again at this example:

★ I'll see you <u>tomorrow</u> then.

Even if it did not contain the adverb <u>tomorrow</u> you would still be able to guess that it was about the future:

★ I'll see you _____ then.

Why? How can we tell? It is to do with the tense of the verbs. 'I'll' is short for 'I will' and from around the age of three we learn to recognise that 'I will' sometimes refers to something that will happen in the future.

Look at the sentences in the chart below. All of them have had their adverbs of time removed. See if you can still work out whether they are talking about the past, present or future. Also, have a guess at what the missing adverb might be.

	Sentence	Tense	Missing adverb
1	The doctor called _____.		
2	We're enjoying the book we're _____ studying.		
3	We had hoped to visit the zoo _____.		
4	This cream we bought _____ tastes off.		
5	I hope you'll contact us again ___.		

Follow-on : We also show whether we mean past, present or future by the way we change (or inflect) the verb. Look at these short sentences and decide for each one whether it refers to the past, present or future. There are no adverbs (like <u>later</u> or <u>yesterday</u>) to help you – so how do you work out what the tense is?

1	I will eat my soup.		5	The tank is full.
2	She ate her soup.		6	She filled the tank.
3	He was thinking.		7	I'll fill the tank.
4	They are thinking.		8	She's filling the tank.

Now for each one, try writing it in a different tense by changing the verb. Here's an example of number one to show you how:

★ I am eating my soup.   = present tense

Key point: In English we show whether we mean past, present or future using adverbs of time (e.g. 'I am going tomorrow.'). We also sometimes inflect the verbs: 'I enjoy music' (present), 'I enjo<u>yed</u> the music' (past).

COPYMASTER  **Tense in texts**

25 Tense in texts

Learning objective:
to look at the effect different tenses have in texts

A TENSE MOMENTS

Many texts that we read in school are written in the past tense, but not all of them are. Look at this list of texts and decide whether you think they will be set in the past, present or future tense.

1 autobiographies
2 fire escape instructions
3 recipes
4 newspaper articles
5 guide books to a famous city
6 horoscopes in a newspaper or magazine

★ Which did you find easiest?
★ Which was most difficult?

Follow-on: Now choose six of the following mystery texts (more if you want). For each one try to work out:

★ what type of text it is
★ what it might be about
★ which words helped you to work this out
★ who it might be aimed at
★ what tense it is mostly written in (write down two or three examples to show this).

Mystery texts

A It came slowly towards the crowd, its eyes glaring, its teeth bared. The people in the crowd stood stock-still, frozen with fear while ...

B And so it came to pass that on the fourth day the men, women and children came out from the city into the valley below and ...

C Just can't help myself –
It's you, it's you, it's you –
You're the one ooh I need ...

D I am 16 years of age and just about to leave school after taking GCSE examinations. I am interested ...

E To release the cylinder block, first slacken off the camshaft chain tensioner. Then unscrew and remove the single bolt at the rear ...

F Lovely Eleanor, 18, is training to be an air-hostess and tells us that she can't wait to fly ...

G Didn't do much today. Anne came round in the afternoon and we just sat around and talked ...

H Pinchas Zukerman began his mastery of the violin when he was eight. Two years later he won a scholarship ...

I Now, when the little dwarf heard that he was to dance a second time before the Queen he was so proud that ...

J With their album already flying high, the band are planning a number of gigs ...

K I *know* how difficult it must be for you – but be patient because in just a few weeks' time we'll be together ...

L Stir in the sugar with a swift motion and simmer over a very low heat, adding more milk if necessary ...

M After last month's fun and games, you're due for a slow down. Watch out for some odd events next week ...

N And what's more, your cat will simply love the juicy flavour of ...

O In case of emergency, press the red button and wait until the machine stops. Do not ...

P Your postal order is enclosed herewith. We regret any inconvenience caused by our inability to send the goods you require ...

> **Key point –** The clues to a text's tense lies in the verbs and adverbs. Some texts are more likely to use the past tense; some the present tense; some the future tense.

26 Adjectives

A DESCRIBING WORDS

You have already seen how important nouns are – words like 'table', 'hope' and 'Edinburgh'. They allow us to label the world, to give names to things. **Adjectives** help us to make our descriptions of nouns more precise.

Look at this simple sentence:

★ The <u>woman</u> sat on the <u>chair</u>.

Add an adjective or two and you can begin to give greater detail or atmosphere:

★ The <u>old</u> woman sat on the <u>rickety</u> chair.
★ The <u>unhappy</u> woman sat on the <u>comfortable</u> chair.

Adjectives include colours (blue), shades (dark), textures (rough), and states of mind (happy).

Take this simple sentence and write five different versions of it by adding two new adjectives each time. The ✳ shows you the slot where the adjective could fit before each noun.

★ My ✳ dog lay on the ✳ carpet.

B SHELL CHALLENGE

Now test your ability to use adjectives precisely. On the right is a photograph of sea-shells. Each one is different. Pick six shells, and write six brief descriptions, one for each shell. Then challenge a friend to match your descriptions to the picture.

Your description might go like this:

★ My first shell is _____, _____ and _____. Its surface is _____ and its shape is _____.

To highlight the use of adjectives, underline them in a different colour.

Follow-on: Take the Shell Challenge. See if you can identify someone else's choice of shell from the written descriptions they give.

> **Key point –** Adjectives allow us to add detail to the nouns we use. They can make our writing more precise.

27 Adjectives for description

A WRITERS' ADVICE

You already know that adjectives are words we use to add detail to the noun (for example, a <u>hot</u> drink, an <u>unpleasant</u> idea). Perhaps you think that adjectives sound like a useful word class ... but ...

Here is what some writers have said about adjectives:

A 'Nice writing isn't enough. It isn't enough to have smooth and pretty writing. Surprise the reader with the unexpected verb or adjective. Use one startling adjective per page.' (Anne Bernays)

B 'As to the adjective: when in doubt, strike it out.' (Mark Twain)

C 'The adjective is the banana peel of the parts of speech.' (Clifton Fadiman)

1 Use a tick (✔) or cross (✗) to show whether each writer's comments about adjectives are positive or negative.
   A ☐   B ☐   C ☐

2 From the writers' comments, what seems to be the main <u>positive</u> point about adjectives?

3 Can you work out a <u>negative</u> point?

B THE DANGERS OF OVERWRITING

Some writers believe that writing isn't truly creative if it is not crammed with adjectives. Every time they use a noun, they place an adjective before it. Worst of all, many new writers use adjectives they find in the thesaurus and use words that they think sound fancy or impressive.

Look at the text on the right. It is 'overwritten' – it contains too many adjectives. These have been underlined. Imagine that you are an editor at Crowefoot Burrows and Co, a small publishing company. You welcome novels by new writers. Which adjectives would you cut from the first paragraph of this novel, *Face of Darkness*? Write the text out so that it is less cluttered with description, and answer the questions which follow.

> I stood alone on the <u>dark</u>, <u>gloomy</u>, <u>jutting</u> cliff thinking about what <u>faithful</u> <u>old</u> Max had said. Were his <u>secret</u>, <u>whispered</u> words honest? I watched the <u>billowing</u> waves, the <u>rolling</u> hills of <u>wild</u>, <u>crashing</u>, <u>icy</u> water explode beneath my <u>dainty</u> feet. The <u>cool</u>, <u>chill</u>, <u>biting</u> wind lifted and cut into my <u>tightly-wrapped</u>, <u>worried</u> face. I faced an <u>uncertain</u> <u>dark</u> future all alone.
>
> **Jez Nettleton**

1. Write out your revised text.

2. The extract contains 20 adjectives. How many did you cut – all of them, most of them, or a few of them? Write down the number of adjectives you have kept.

3. Write a sentence describing your response to the original text. What was wrong with it? What was right with it?

4. Write a sentence about your own edited version. How have you improved the original? How does it feel different?

Follow-on: Write a letter to the writer of *Face of Darkness* giving advice on how he might improve the opening of his story. You might mention:

★ amount of description

★ choice of vocabulary

★ whether it makes the reader want to read on.

Your letter could begin:

> Dear Jez Nettleton,
> I have just read the opening of your novel and would like to make the following comments ...

> **Key point –** Adjectives are powerful tools for adding detail – but they can be used too much. Too many clog up the reader's response to the text. In using adjectives, make sure that they are serving a precise purpose – otherwise, cut them!

28 Adverbs

A   DESCRIBING THE ACTION

You already know that we can add detail to nouns by using adjectives – for example, take the noun 'house' and simply add an adjective:

★   the <u>old</u> house   or   the house is <u>old</u>

Adverbs have a similar effect, except that they describe verbs rather than nouns.

Take a verb like 'run'. Add a word to describe <u>how</u> someone runs:

★   She runs quickly.
★   He runs strangely.
★   The dog runs madly.

Adverbs often end with -ly which makes them easy to recognise. But some do not – for example, 'fast' and 'soon'.

Take this list of sentences and for each one place an adverb where it seems to fit best. To help you, the main verb in each sentence has been underlined. Some sentences contain more than one verb.

You might decide to add more than one adverb to them.

1. I <u>sat</u> at the edge of the river.
2. The water <u>moved</u> past me.
3. There <u>was</u> a sound.
4. I <u>heard</u> the sound of an engine.
5. It was <u>heading</u> towards me.
6. I <u>pulled</u> in my fishing line and watched.
7. The noise <u>grew</u> louder.
8. The boat was <u>speeding</u> along the river.
9. As it passed, I <u>looked</u> at the name on the boat.
10. It <u>said</u> 'Wave-Maker'.

WORD BANK: ADVERBS

PEACEFULLY   SLUGGISHLY   NOISILY   ANGRILY
GENTLY   HARDLY   SUDDENLY   MASSIVELY
IMMEDIATELY   AUTOMATICALLY   INSTINCTIVELY
QUICKLY   EVEN   CAREFULLY   CRAZILY   RECKLESSLY
MADLY   CLOSELY   SPEEDILY   JUST   MERELY
APPARENTLY   SIMPLY   NERVOUSLY

B | ADVERB TYPES

Adverbs fall into different groups:

MANNER – these tell you how someone does something. For example:

★ happily – he sat <u>happily</u> for hours

★ lazily

★ angrily

TIME – these tell you when something is happening. For example:

★ recently – she's <u>recently</u> moved in

★ still

★ regularly

PLACE – these tell you where something is happening. Notice that they do not have to end with -ly, but they are still adverbs because they add detail to the verb. For example:

★ upstairs – she walked <u>upstairs</u>

★ outside

★ overhead

There are other types of adverbs too, but these are the main groups we use. Look at the adverbs listed below. Decide which group they belong to – manner (M), time (T) or place (P).

1	quickly	4	abroad	7	sadly
2	briefly	5	today	8	somewhere
3	inside	6	rudely	9	immediately

Follow-on: Write two sentences for each type of adverb: two for 'manner', two for 'time' and two for 'place'.

> **Key point –** Adverbs add detail to the verb. They show us when, where, or how something is happening.

29 Conjunctions

Learning objective:
to look at the variety of words you can use to link ideas together

A MAKING LINKS

Conjunctions are words that allow us to join phrases, clauses and sentences together. Without them, our ideas would feel very boring – like this:

★ My homework is finished. I am going to hand it in tomorrow. It was really difficult. It took me ages. I am pleased I've finished it.

(Mark, Year 9)

We asked Mark to rewrite these sentences using conjunctions, so that it flowed more and felt less disjointed. Here is what he came up with:

★ My homework is finished and I am going to hand it in tomorrow. It was really difficult and took me ages, and so I am pleased I've finished it.

Mark says: "This is much more the way I'd speak, except I'd probably say 'I'm' instead of 'I am'. Sometimes though, my written work is criticised for using too many 'ands'."

Take the following text and make it more interesting to read by adding conjunctions from the word bank below. Some hints:

1 You do not have to use a conjunction between every sentence – choose one only when you think it is needed.
2 Try to avoid using 'and' all the time.
3 Sometimes you may want to cut a word or change the order of words to make the sentence flow better.

WORD BANK: CONJUNCTIONS

(THE CONJUNCTIONS WE USE MOST OFTEN ARE LISTED FIRST, FOLLOWED BY MORE ADVANCED TYPES)

AND BUT OR BECAUSE
ALTHOUGH AS IF UNTIL
UNLESS WHILE BEFORE DESPITE

It was raining. The sky looked heavy. The trees swayed. They lost their leaves in the strong wind. The pavements hissed. The rain fell onto them. The gutters filled up. The drains worked overtime. I sat at the window. I watched the miserable scene.

B | ANDS OFF!

Mark mentioned that he was sometimes told to use 'and' less in his written work. Why, do you think?

Linking sentences with 'and' all the time can become as boring as never using a conjunction. Look at this extract from Vicky's story about a wife and husband after an argument:

> Mrs Fletcher sat there and wondered if he would come home and she made herself a cup of tea. Then there was a knock at the door and when she opened it she saw her husband and he said 'Can I come in?' And she thought for a minute and then she said 'Yes' and so he came into the room and sat down. For a few seconds there was silence and then she said 'Do you want some tea?' and he said 'Yes please' and they started to get along better again.

1. Read it through again. If you were Vicky's teacher, what advice would you give her? Write down your comments.

2. Rewrite the paragraph cutting conjunctions, adding conjunctions, or changing conjunctions, so that you make the text read better.

Follow-on: *Either* (a) redraft a page from one of your recent assignments, using conjunctions to improve the flow of it; *or* (b) as practice, write a paragraph on one of the topics below, using a variety of conjunctions from the word bank:

★ a fire alarm during a lesson
★ an invasion of ants in your kitchen

> **Key point –** Conjunctions are important words for linking phrases, clauses and sentences together. Used carefully, they also make your text more interesting to read.

Prepositions plus

30 Prepositions plus

Learning objective:
to learn about prepositions

A | WHERE IS IT?

Prepositions are frequently tiny words. We can easily forget how important they are in telling someone **where** someone or something is.
Some of the most useful prepositions are shown in the word bank.

**WORD BANK:
PREPOSITIONS OF PLACE**

IN   ON   UNDER   THROUGH
BEHIND   BETWEEN UNDERNEATH
BEFORE   BESIDE   INTO   WITH
NEAR   WITHIN   OFF   ACROSS
DOWN   AT

Look at the picture below of a room. Then look at the list of questions which follow. See if you can answer the questions **without** using any of the words in the word bank.

1. Where is the cat?
2. Where is the table?
3. Where is the skull?
4. Where is the grandfather clock?
5. Where is the large spider's-web?
6. Where is the telephone?
7. Where is the pile of books?

B DEMONSTRATIVE DEMO

As you can see, without prepositions it becomes difficult to tell someone exactly where something is. It is easier, though, when we are actually with the person. We can point to the object and use a demonstrative pronoun. This is a word which 'demonstrates' where something is.

Follow-on: This sketch uses lots of prepositions and demonstrative pronouns. It is a discussion between two people. One of them is proving very slow to understand. Read it, and then try to continue it for ten or more lines. Use as many prepositions and demonstrative pronouns as you can, and underline them.

Removals

(Man in overalls walks into the kitchen)

A: <u>This</u> is the stuff you want moving then, is it?

B: What?

A: <u>This</u> stuff here?

B: Moving where?

A: Moving <u>to</u> the new house?

B: Which new house?

A: The one <u>behind</u> the – you know – <u>up</u> the main street, <u>round</u> the corner, <u>up</u> <u>at</u> the back <u>of</u> the gasworks.

B: I think you must have made a mistake.

A: <u>This</u> is 32 Oaklands Avenue?

B: Yes.

A: Then <u>this</u> must be the stuff we're moving – <u>this</u> lot here?

B: Now wait a minute ...

> **Key point –** Prepositions help us to tell someone where something is. Face-to-face demonstratives have a similar function – they allow us to show more precisely which object we are referring to. In writing, you need to use them with care.

1 What does 'inflection' allow us to do?

2 Give an example of inflection using these two words:

★ car

★ eat

3 Look at this sentence:

★ I saw your auntie swing that old coat over her head.

From the sentence:

a) write down a noun

b) write down a verb

c) say whether the tense of the verb you have chosen is past or present

d) write down an adjective

e) write down a preposition

f) write down a demonstrative pronoun.

Make a note of your score on the Progress Chart. Use the Homework File to revise any areas you feel uncertain about. Remember that it is more important to be able to use different classes of words precisely than to be able to name them.

Discourse structure: Organising whole texts

AIMS:

★ to look at the way larger texts are organised – what the National Curriculum for English defines as 'discourse structure'

★ to explore some differences between different varieties of English

In this section you will:

★ learn about paragraphing – an important way of organising whole texts

★ look at the way different types of texts have different openings and endings

★ explore what standard English is – and why it has so much influence

★ investigate the differences between spoken and written texts.

Remember:

★ the Homework File has activity sheets so that you can practise all the skills you learn

★ there is a self-assessment test at the end of the section, so you can chart your progress.

32 Paragraphing

Learning objective:
to become more confident in using paragraphs

A | **THE PURPOSE OF PARAGRAPHS**

Paragraphs help us to organise our ideas in larger texts. They:

★ make it easier for the reader to follow your ideas by showing where one topic ends and another one begins

★ make a text more structured and therefore easier to read.

Look what happens when you read a piece of text which has not been clearly organised:

Rats

Rats will eat any human food. Their favourite foods are fruit, peanut butter, and fresh meat. They don't seem so keen on cheese. Many rats have got a taste for warfarin which is used to poison them. They will actually eat through a shopping basket to get a taste of warfarin. Humans have had to find new poisons. Rats originally came from eastern Asia but their population grew quickly wherever there were human beings. They plagued most ancient civilisations. Before 1727 there were mainly plagues of black rats. Then a new wave of large brown rats moved in from Russia. There are now almost no black rats in the world except in the hot climates of the tropics which the brown rat hates. Rats reproduce very quickly. Female rats have about five litters per year. Each litter might contain up to 23 babies. One pair of rats could have 350,000,000 relatives in three years if they all survived. Scientists have found that rats with brothers and sisters seem more stable and contented than single rats.

Decide how you would reorganise this text to make it easier for the reader.

① Work out how many paragraphs you would use by thinking about the different topics the text contains.

② Label each paragraph (for example, 'rat family life').

③ Which order would you place the paragraphs in?

Compare your answers with a friend's.

B | PARAGRAPH STYLES

We vary the way we use paragraphs according to our purpose. In a formal essay you might aim to use just two or three paragraphs to a page, each one covering a new topic. On the other hand, in newspapers you might expect to find lots of very short paragraphs, each one perhaps containing just one sentence. Why?

Journalists want you to absorb information quickly and easily. They want to keep their stories moving. Short paragraphs can make it simpler to follow a text. Also, until recently, newspapers were edited by cutting text using razor blades. The page would be pasted together and the text cut to fit. The most important information was put at the top of the story. The background information and quotations were placed at the bottom – and was the first to be cut if a story was too long. Provided they were short, whole paragraphs could be sliced out from the foot of a story.

Look at an example from your own choice of newspaper, or see the magazine article in Copymaster 32 of the Homework File.

1 What different topics are covered in the story?
2 Does it need so many paragraphs?

Follow-on: Take the 'Rats' text from activity A and write it more clearly. Organise the text into a sensible order and use paragraphs to help the reader know when new ideas begin.

> **Key point –** Paragraphs help us to make texts clearer for the reader by showing where new topics begin. Newspapers use very short paragraphs (often just a sentence long). In formal contexts (for example, English assignments) we often make paragraphs longer than that.

COPYMASTER 32A–C
 **Openings and closings**

33 Openings and closings

Learning objective:
to compare the way writers start and end their texts.

A STARTING POINTS AND LAST WORDS

In some texts, you don't have much choice over how you begin or end.
There is a rule or convention about what you should write. See if you can
work out which types of texts the following openings and endings belong to.

1. Dear Marge ...

2. Once upon a time ...

3. Thursday, 13 November

   I ...

4. All the best,

   Kate.

5. Serve warm on small plates.

6. 1: EXT.

   NIGHT. A STREET.

7. Rest in peace.

B STORY OPENINGS

An expert on writing short stories gives this advice: 'An effective short story
is one that hooks us with the first sentence and keeps us reading until the
end. A greater short story is one which makes us feel that the effort has
been worthwhile.' (Michael Baldwin, *The Way to Write Short Stories*)
Look at these short-story openings. Give each one a rating on a scale of 1–5
(5 being most readable). Then try to say why you would or would not want
to read on.

1. The first time I robbed Tiffany's it was raining.

2. 'You got three quarters of an hour,' said the porter.

3. It was nearly midnight. There was a frosty stare to the big stars and the
   moon above the farmhouse gleamed like a splash of whitewash.

4. Mr Francis O'Reilly, known to a wide circle of enemies as Foxer, lay on his
   narrow prison bed, thinking of old age and death.

5. She terrified me. She looked like a fly.

As you look at each story opening, try to be precise about what you like/dislike. You might mention: characters, words, atmosphere, tension, surprises, detail.

C   LAST WORDS

People often have mixed feelings about getting to the end of a story. We might be keen to see what finally happens to the characters, but we can also feel a sense of sadness that our time with the text is over. Short-story writers often want us to feel baffled, or disturbed, by their endings.

Look at the following story endings. Using the list of 'story genres' below, see what you can work out about the type or genre of each story.

1. He said, 'I'll be off then.' And was gone.

2. She dwelt in poverty till she died, because she did not heed the instruction given to her by the tree.

3. Now it is May. Twilight is setting in, evening is come. Soon it will be dark. I will then start to sing or, as human beings call it, warble.

4. Never more alone. My heart bursting, a blackness in front of my eyes. I hope it won't hurt too much.

5. And to this day, narcissus flowers can be found, growing wild in the woods and sprouting round the banks of a silent pool.

STORY GENRES

WAR   HORROR   GHOST
STORY   ROMANTIC FICTION
FAIRY TALE   MYTH/LEGEND
FANTASY   THRILLER

Try to explain which clues in each ending helped you to make your decision. You might mention: words, sentence structure, characters, other texts you are reminded of.

Follow-on: Put together a collection of story openings and endings – a sentence or two from each. Then see if a friend can match the two parts up – the beginning of one story to its ending.

Key point – There are conventions or rules for some beginnings and endings. In fiction, we can often work out the genre of a text from its opening or ending.

COPYMASTER  **What is standard English?**

34 What is standard English?

A LANGUAGE VARIETIES

Walk into a supermarket and you will see dozens of varieties of cola, lots of varieties of crisps and biscuits, an amazing range of breakfast cereals. Just imagine if the English language was on the supermarket shelves. Again, there would be dozens, even hundreds, of varieties. You would be able to recognise almost all of them as English, but they would each have something different about them.

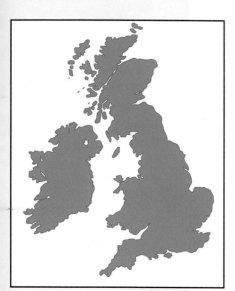

Look at these examples. Each word or phrase comes from a different region of Britain. For each one, try to:

★ say which of the expressions **you** would use
★ guess where you think some of the others might come from (which parts of Britain).

1	Fool gowk April Gowk April Noddy April Fool
2	goosebob goosegog gooseberry goosegob grozer
3	she-cat queen ewe female cat sheeder betty cat
4	leery leer clammed hungered hungry
5	chuck throw fling hain heave yack pelt swail hoy

B STANDARD ENGLISH

All over Britain there are different words to describe things. For example, in Cornwall and parts of the Midlands a pond is a 'pool'; in the Northwest it is a 'pit'; in North Staffordshire it is a 'mere'. A bread roll might be a cob, a bun or a stotty, depending on where you live. An alleyway may be a ginnel, a snicket, or even a snickleway. This variety of words and expressions is a reminder that English is made from different **dialects**.

One dialect is generally seen as more important than all the others because it has more prestige and power: standard English. This is the form of English you will find in dictionaries, encyclopaedias, official reports, instruction books, and so on.

Look back at the lists of words in activity A. If you were putting a dictionary together, which word from each of the five lists would you choose to include? Probably it will be the one that most people will know – the one that belongs to standard English.

Write down the *five* words you would choose.

Follow-on: Look at the maze of words below and the five standard English words that are underlined. Underneath these five words, write down three dialect words with a similar meaning. Then place a tick by the dialect form you would be most likely to use at home. For example:

★ <u>Active</u>
fidgety
on the go ✔
wick

WORD MAZE

WORKMATE   TAMP   US BOTH   GRANSHER   US BE

GRAMF

BUTTY   BOUNCE   PAL

WE TWO

GRANFER

STOT

WE BIN

DAP   US TWO   WE ARE

MATE

GRANDAD

WE AM   THE TWO ON US

Key point – Dialects are varieties of English, giving us different words and expressions. The dialect used in most writing is called standard English.

  **Spoken and written English**

35 Spoken and written English

Learning objective:
to look at some of the main differences between spoken and written English

A | SPOT THE SPEECH

Here are two stories. One of them was spoken aloud by one friend to another. The other was written in an English lesson. Can you tell which is which?

★ Text A: Michelle

> I had a tip off that there were some stolen antiques in a house called Hazard House. That morning I went to the house to have a look around. When I arrived at the house at around ten a.m., the door was not locked. I went in. It was very dark and I switched my torch on. I noticed some spiders and lots of cobwebs. I pushed my way in and suddenly thought that I could hear a dog. I paused. I listened. There it was again. I froze to the spot and wondered what to do next.

★ Text B: Rebecca

> It was about five o'clock and I was at the sports centre and I was er waiting for my dad because we were going to you know play tennis and he'd got a court booked but it was about five past so I was wondering if he'd forgotten or something or couldn't get a court so I rang him up and he said he was just leaving so I started to run round the track and when he came he went and got the court and while we were playing I just saw this heard this ambulance and then a police car.

Look at each of the following statements and decide which text it best fits – written (W) or spoken (S) or both (B).

1. The sentences are clearly organised.
2. Punctuation is used to make meaning clearer for the reader.
3. Sentences are linked by basic conjunctions, like 'and' and adverbs like 'so'.
4. The sentence structure makes it feel like a written story.
5. Tone of voice and pauses are used to structure the ideas.
6. The vocabulary is very straightforward.
7. The writer uses words to create atmosphere.
8. The text contains interruptions, making it seem like spoken language.

B | CONTEXTS

Sometimes we need to communicate using speech; sometimes the communication has to be in writing. Look at the list of communication contexts below, and decide whether you think each one is better suited to speech (S) or writing (W) or either (E). Then try to say why you think speech or writing is more suitable.

	Context	S, W or E?	Why?
1	Reporting a robbery to the police		
2	Complaining about something you have just bought		
3	Thanking a distant relative for a birthday present		
4	Booking a seat at the cinema		
5	Giving a complicated recipe to someone		
6	Telling someone you love them		
7	Telling the story of your life		
8	Telling someone what to do with all your money once you're dead		
9	Telling someone what to buy at the supermarket		
10	Explaining how to service a car		

Follow-on: Look again at activity A. The spoken text would be structured by the speaker's voice and pauses. Now take the text and rewrite it as if it was the beginning of a written story. Reorganise it and use punctuation to give it greater clarity to a reader rather than a listener.

> **Key point –** Spoken and written English are often different. One form is not better than the other: they have different purposes. In thinking about our purpose and audience, we have to decide which form is more appropriate.

Self-assessment page: Discourse structure

Discourse structure means the organisation of whole texts. Use this page to chart your progress. Remember that any parts you find especially difficult can be reviewed in the additional units in the Homework File. Use the Progress Chart to track how you do.

1 In one sentence, say what the purpose of using paragraphs is.

2 Name a context where you might find very short paragraphs.

3 Name a context where you might find more lengthy paragraphs.

4 Which statement best describes what standard English is?

a) correct pronunciation

b) the most important variety of English

c) the way educated people write

d) written, not spoken, language

5 Our language varies according to the situation we are in. In general, which is more formal – speech or writing?

Punctuation:
Helping the reader to follow your ideas

AIMS:

★ to see how punctuation is an essential part of written grammar – not something separate from it

★ to look at how punctuation can make your ideas much clearer for a reader to follow

In this section you will learn:

★ why we use punctuation in written English

★ what happens if we leave punctuation out

★ how capital letters and full stops are the essential punctuation ingredients

★ how other punctuation marks can give your ideas greater clarity and precision

★ how to punctuate speech

★ how to use the two types of apostrophe.

Remember:

★ the Homework File has activity sheets so that you can practise all the skills you learn

★ there is a self-assessment test at the end of the section, so you can chart your progress.

37 Punctuation: Why do we need it?

Learning objective:
to clarify why we need punctuation

A   PUNCTUATION MYTHS

People have mixed ideas about why we use punctuation. Look at this collection of comments from a Year 8 class:

> Commas help you to know when to breathe.

> Full stops let you stop your sentences from getting too long.

> Exclamation marks mean someone is shouting.

> I've got no idea what a semi-colo looks like, let alone wha you use it for.

Punctuation actually has a simple purpose. It helps us to communicate our ideas clearly in writing. We quickly get used to this. Look what would happen, for example, if we didn't use spaces between words. Try reading this text and work out what it says:

> Afterawhileithoughtitwouldbeagoodideatogohomeihadspent
> suchalongtimeatvickyshousethatiwasafraidmymumwouldhav
> eforgottenwhoiwasidbettergonow

B | SENDING SIGNALS

When we read a text, we take it for granted that:

★ capital letters signal the start of sentences or the names of people, places and products

★ full stops signal the end of sentences

★ speech marks show us the words a person actually speaks or thinks

★ question marks signal questions.

This all seems obvious. But look at the text below. It contains no clues about where ideas start and end. It isn't clear which parts are spoken and which are description. The only clues to help you are capital letters for the two people involved and apostrophes to show where words have been compressed (for example, 'couldn't' and 'I'd') or to show possession (for example, 'Vicky's house'). Work out what the writer is saying.

After a while I thought it would be a good idea to go home I had spent such a long time at Vicky's house that I was afraid my mum would have forgotten who I was I'd better go now then Vicky I said what she said already yes I said why I couldn't face an argument so I just got my coat and waved goodbye Vicky was fine about it when I saw her next day we're still friends

Follow-on: Using only capital letters and full stops (but no other punctuation marks), write the text out so that the beginning and end of sentences become more clear.

> **Key point –** Punctuation is all about clarity: it helps us to communicate our ideas more clearly.

38 Basic punctuation

Learning objective:
to make sure you understand the use of basic punctuation marks

A ADDING CLARITY

Remember: all punctuation is designed to help you express your ideas more clearly. It isn't about knowing when to breathe. It isn't there to stop sentences getting too long. It is about shaping sentences so that they are clear for the reader to follow.

Look at the sentences below. They have different meanings according to where the punctuation is placed. Try to describe how the meaning of A is different from B in each pair of sentences.

1 A I hate boys like you. I find them revolting.

   B I hate boys. Like you, I find them revolting.

2 A The King prayed half an hour after he was beheaded.

   B The King prayed half an hour. After he was beheaded.

3 A Lonely librarian seeks a friend who reads.

   B Lonely librarian seeks a friend. Who reads?

B BACK TO BASICS

Read this brief guide to basic punctuation, and then practise using each of the punctuation marks below.

Capital letters

★ show the start of sentences

★ show the names of people (Fred), places (Halifax), and products (Pepsi).

Full stops

★ show the end of sentences. They tell the reader that this is the end of one idea. They are the most important way of giving clear meaning to a text.

Commas

★ break up items in a list (for example, 'The day was cool, breezy and misty.' 'Don't forget to buy sugar, flour, margarine, eggs and chocolate chips.')

* help the reader to understand the text by creating an island of words ('The man, Mr Samson, approached me.' 'The wheel, in fact, had stopped.')
* separate clauses ('After you left, everything went wrong.' 'Looking really happy, she set off to the bank.')
* create a gap before a name ('Hi, Sally. Hello, Pete.')
* give clarity in speech punctuation ('"It was cold," she said. He replied, "I know."')

Question marks

* show questions – even when there is only one word ('Are you okay?' 'Happy?')

Exclamation marks

* show emotion or excitement ('Only one week left! Hurry!' 'Ouch! That really hurt!')

Follow-on: Look at this text, which has no punctuation. Use the basic punctuation marks above to give it clarity.

People sometimes think that lifts are recent inventions in fact they were used as long ago as 1743 in that year a lift was installed in france in the palace of versailles in fact it was used to connect two bedrooms in the nineteenth century lifts really became popular in new york the inventor of the passenger lift mr otis showed people that lifts were safe and that they should stop being afraid he actually cut through a cord holding the lift shock horror why didn't the lift fall to the ground because mr otis had designed special teeth to grip the lift and hold it in place once people were confident the building of skyscrapers soon followed the passenger lift was born

Key point – Basic punctuation marks help us to make meanings clear for readers. They allow us to show where one topic starts and ends. The most important punctuation marks, therefore, are capital letters and full stops.

COPYMASTER 38 A/B

Speech punctuation

39 Speech punctuation

Learning objective:
to clarify how speech punctuation is used

A | SPEECH MARKS

Speech marks (or direct speech) have a simple purpose – to show us what someone is saying. Without them, texts can seem very confusing. Look at this extract from a story written by Saira in Year 8. The punctuation – including speech marks – has been left out. See if you can work out who is saying what.

> So I said what's going on and Craig said nothing nothing I said yes he said fine I said.

You could write this with speech punctuation in different ways. It all depends who says what:

Version A

'So,' I said, 'what's going on?' and Craig said, 'Nothing.'
'Nothing?' I said.
'Yes,' he said.
'Fine,' I said.

Version B

So I said, 'What's going on?' and Craig said nothing.
'Nothing?' I said.
'Yes,' he said.
'Fine,' I said.

Version C

So I said, 'What's going on?' and Craig said nothing. Nothing!
I said, 'Yes.'
He said, 'Fine I said.'

1 Which of these versions of the extract do you think is the one Saira intended?
2 How is the meaning different in each example?

B DIRECT SPEECH RULES

Here are the essential rules of direct speech. The example below gives you more hints on making speech clear.

1 Use speech marks around the words a person actually says.

2 Place each new speaker's words on a different line, as if you were beginning a new paragraph.

3 Start the spoken words of a following speaker with a capital letter.

4 Always place a punctuation mark at the end of the speech marks, on the inside. This might be a full stop, question mark, exclamation mark or comma.

Example

'Hello,' said Tricia.

Mike replied, 'Hi.'

'Are you okay?' she asked.

'Fine,' Mike said, 'just a bit fed up, that's all.'

★ Capital letter at the start of the speaker's words

★ Punctuation marks at the end of her words – on the inside

★ Comma shows that the sentence continues

★ If the sentence carries on, use a small letter, even after a question mark

★ If the speaker's words fall into two sections, the second section does not need a capital letter

Follow-on: Try using direct speech (speech marks) to make this short extract clearer.

> Hello said Debbie. Hi said Sam. Everything okay said Debbie. Not really said Sam. Oh said Debbie.

Key point – Speech marks or direct speech enable us to show clearly what someone is saying.

COPYMASTER  **Advanced punctuation**

40 Advanced punctuation

Learning objective:
to see how using advanced punctuation marks can further improve your written work

A ADVANCED CHECKLIST

The most important punctuation mark is the full stop. It is what we use to show the end of a unit of meaning, the end of a sentence. But apart from basic punctuation marks – full stops, commas, question marks and exclamation marks – there are others that are needed less often. Used well, they can give greater subtlety or precision to your written expression.

The colon (:)

★ used chiefly before a list.

   ('You will need the following: raincoat, sandwiches, money and tickets.')

★ used within sentences to suggest that another idea or group of words will follow. It can create suspense or a feeling of expectation.

   ('The old man continued on his journey down the dusty road: he knew he was almost at the end.')

   TIP: If you are unsure, use a full stop instead.

The semi-colon (;)

★ used to separate longer items (usually phrases or clauses) in a list, to give clarity.

   ('You will need: a pair of old boots that have been cleaned; a pack of cheese sandwiches in a waterproof box; something to write with such as a pencil; a clean handkerchief.')

★ sometimes we use it within sentences to separate clauses; this can give sentences a feeling of balance or careful thought.

   ('I saw the criminal; he saw me.' 'The cat looked ill; I called the vet.')

   TIP: The semi-colon usually 'feels' like something between a full stop and a comma. It often fits where we might use the word 'and'. If unsure, use a full stop.

The dash (—)

★ useful for more informal writing, or to give a feeling of haste or urgency.

   ('Quick – call an ambulance.' 'It's here – the circus has arrived.')

★ you can also use two dashes to create islands of words within a sentence. ('The glass – chipped and dirty – began to roll across the table.')

TIP: Used too often, the dash can create a very informal tone.

The hyphen (-)

★ shows a line-break, where a word continues on the next line (e.g. dis-agrees

★ used to join words together to create a single meaning. ('They look like big-game hunters.' Look at how the meaning would be different if you did not use the hyphen here.)

TIP: Some people use hyphens in words which other people leave as two separate words and other people run together as one (ice cream, ice-cream, icecream). Check a good dictionary if you are unsure.

Follow-on: Look at the following text which contains examples of the use of each of these advanced punctuation marks. The examples are numbered. In your own words, try to explain why the writer has used that punctuation mark at that point.

It was cold; it was dark; I felt lonely (1). I stood beneath the street-lamp (2), waiting for something – something bad (3). I listened. Something – I wasn't sure what – had begun to move (4). I peered hard into the darkness: 'it' peered back at me (5).

Key point – Advanced punctuation provides you with more language tools for expressing ideas more clearly and precisely.

 COPYMASTER 40 A/B

 NEXT STEP **Apostrophes 1: Compression**

41 Apostrophes 1: Compression

A | APOSTROPHE PAIRS

People often get confused about apostrophes. They begin to think you have to sprinkle them over all your sentences – like vinegar on fish and chips.

Using apostrophes ought to be easy because there are two simple rules. This unit looks at the first; the next unit explores the second. Get the rules clear in your mind, and they will help you to communicate your meaning clearly.

Apostrophes for compression

★ Rule – We use apostrophes when we squeeze two words together to make one compressed word:

Look at the examples below. Words that could be compressed are underlined. Write the sentences out using apostrophes to show the way you have squeezed words together.

1. I <u>did not</u> notice that he was watching me.
2. I hope I <u>was not</u> doing anything wrong.
3. He said <u>he had</u> seen me breaking a window.
4. I said that he <u>can not</u> have seen me.
5. <u>It is</u> really unfair the way I always get blamed.

Compare your rewritten sentences with the original examples. Try to say in two or three sentences how the two sets 'feel different'. When might you speak using the words separately? When would you be likely to use them compressed, with apostrophes?

B | DECOMPRESSION CHAMBER

Now take a look at the passage below. It contains seven compressed words – but the apostrophes have been left out. See if you can find all seven words and write them down correctly punctuated.

> Were really looking forward to the end of term. Its been ages since weve had any holidays. I couldnt stand the thought of carrying on with lessons much longer. Theres going to be parties and all sorts, Im told. Itll be great.

Follow-on: Look again at the paragraph above. Read it to yourself with all seven compressed words written as two words (for example, 'it's' as 'it has'). How does the text feel different? Try to think up some words of advice about when to use compressed forms of words and when to leave them as separate words. Use these situations as a starting point:

★ talking to friends

★ in a business letter

★ in an essay about a book you have studied

★ in a formal speech

★ on the telephone to an important person

> **Key point –** We use apostrophes when we compress two words together to make one.

42 Apostrophes 2: Possession

Learning objective:
to learn about the way we use apostrophes to show that something belongs to someone or something

A | BEING POSSESSIVE

People find this use of apostrophes more confusing because there are one or two odd rules. Before you start, you need to be clear in your mind about why we use apostrophes for compression. If that unit does not make complete sense, work on the activities in the Homework File, read the Glossary, and practise!

Apostrophes for possession show that something belongs to someone or something. Meet Rex, our friendly mascot for this unit. Surrounding him are his favourite objects.

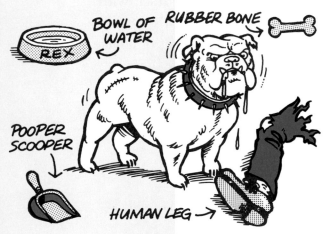

If we were writing about Rex's possessions, we would simply say:

★ 'Here is Rex's bowl of water'. 'There is Rex's rubber bone'. And so on.

Look at the cartoon characters below. Look at the possessions list. Match each item (in the right-hand list) to the person who probably owns it (in the left-hand list). Then write a sentence to describe who owns what, using apostrophes for possession.

Write your sentences using these subject-starters:

1 I saw ...   2 They noticed ...
3 We laughed at ...   4 I was terrified by ...
5 Everyone was surprised by ...

OWNERS
1 Chuck
2 Samantha
3 The unhappy man
4 The angry woman
5 The magician

POSSESSIONS
A unsuccessful magic trick
B long face
C rage
D unusual hobby
E new car

B   PLUS PLURALS

Look at these two sentences:

★ I enjoyed the <u>boy's</u> talk in assembly today.

★ I enjoyed the <u>boys'</u> talk in assembly today.

Q: How many boys talked in the first example?   A: One.

Q: How many boys talked in the second example?   A: More than one.

We can tell by looking at the position of the apostrophe. If it is at the end of **boy**, it means there is just one boy. If it is at the end of the plural, **boys**, then there were more than one.

Read these examples and decide whether the 'owner' is S (singular – just one) or P (plural – more than one). Don't guess: look closely at the position of the apostrophe. It is there to clarify the meaning.

1 I hated the dog's howling.

2 The soldiers' boots were muddy on the mat.

3 We visited my friend's school.

4 I hope the babies' crying will soon stop.

One final hint: some names already end in 's' and it can seem odd to add an apostrophe + s to show that they own something:

★ Tess's shoes or Tess' shoes?

The best rule is: if you hear the extra 's' after the apostrophe when you say it, write it down to help the reader.

Follow-on: Think up six sentences containing apostrophes for possession (three singular, three plural). Write them down, using the apostrophe to make their meaning clear.

Key point – Apostrophes for possession, like other punctuation marks, make meanings clearer – this time, what belongs to whom.

Use this page to look at your strengths and weaknesses in this section. Use the units in the Homework File to develop your skills and knowledge further, and use the Progress Chart to track your development.

1 Which of these statements best describes the purpose of punctuation?

    a) it shows us when to breathe

    b) it makes texts look clearer

    c) it makes the meaning of writing clearer to the reader

    d) it shows that you know how to write properly

2 Why do we need capital letters and full stops in writing?

3 What are the two uses of apostrophes?

4 Write down a sentence which shows both types of apostrophe in use.

This checklist is intended as a quick reference guide to terms used in the book, plus some other important grammatical words.

Active and passive – two ways of using verbs. One emphasises the subject of a sentence; the other can create an impersonal tone:

Mary then mixed the hydrogen with the potassium. (Active – Mary did it)
The hydrogen and potassium were then mixed. (Passive – it isn't clear who did the mixing)

Adjective – a word which gives more information about a noun or pronoun – e.g. the <u>old</u> horse; she is <u>special</u>.

Adverb – a word which gives more information about a verb – e.g. the boy ran <u>clumsily</u>. Adverbs can tell us about manner (slowly), time (yesterday) and place (nearby).

Apostrophe – a punctuation mark used to clarify two types of meaning:
1 It shows when two words have been compressed (did + not = didn't). We use this type of expression more in informal situations.
2 It shows that something belongs to someone (Sarah's money). The apostrophe can inform the reader about whether the noun is singular (just one) or plural (more than one), according to its position. For example, in "I noticed the horse's bad behaviour" the placing of the apostrophe after <u>horse</u> shows that there is just one horse. In "I noticed the horses' bad behaviour" the apostrophe is placed after the plural, <u>horses</u>, so that there is more than one horse.

Auxiliary verb – a verb form we put before the main verb to change its meaning – such as number and tense:

auxiliary verb/s	main verb
is	eating
are	eating
has been	eating
will	eat
might	eat

The most common auxiliary verbs are <u>to be</u> (is/was/are/am/were) and <u>to have</u> (has/had/have).

Clause – a group of words formed around a verb. They are used to make up sentences. This compound sentence contains two clauses linked by <u>and</u>:

I worried about my grandma and *she worried about me.*

The complex sentence below also contains two clauses. One is the **main clause** (it carries the main information). The second is the **subordinate** or **dependent clause** (it gives background detail):

The bullfighter left the ring, dragging his cape behind him.

Colon – punctuation mark which shows that something else follows within the sentence.

Comma – punctuation mark used to separate items in a list, or clarify meaning within sentences.

Connective – a word or phrase that helps us to make connections between different ideas in a text. Typical examples include: <u>on the other hand</u>, <u>however</u>, <u>in fact</u>. Each of these hints that the sentence or paragraph which follows will connect with what has gone before – giving a different argument (<u>on the other hand/however</u>) or adding more information (<u>in fact</u>).

Conjunction – a word used for joining sentences and ideas together. The most commonly-used examples are <u>and</u>, <u>but</u>, <u>or</u>, <u>because</u>.

Dashes – punctuation marks used to add information, or – sometimes – to bracket off ideas.

Demonstrative pronoun – a word which demonstrates where something is: <u>That</u> candle! <u>This</u> pitchfork! We use demonstratives mostly when we are actually with someone. Then we can be sure that they can see what we are referring to. If they are not with us, we need to use prepositions precisely.

Dialect – a regional variety of English. Just as there are different varieties of breakfast cereal, some sweet, some healthy, some crunchy, some smooth, so English has varieties of words and grammatical constructions. The word *hedgehog* is used in some regions; *urchin* is preferred in other places. The sentence *I will teach you that later* is the normal way of speaking in some places; in others you might say, *I'll learn you that later*. Dialects remind us of our roots – the way language has developed differently in different regions over hundreds of years. In formal situations and in writing, standard English is usually used.

Direct speech – a speaker's words or thoughts, placed within speech marks.

Dynamic and stative verbs – dynamic verbs describe actions (to hit, to travel, to jump). Stative verbs describe states of mind (to think, to hope, to be).

Exclamation mark – punctuation mark used to show urgency or emotion.

Full stop – punctuation mark used to mark the ends of sentences.

Genre – a type or category of writing (e.g. some fiction categories include science fiction, horror and crime writing).

Grammar – the way words are put together to communicate meaning. From an early age we learn about the rules of word-order. In English you can say: "I like this porridge" but not "I like this porridge not". We learn that certain words go together in certain ways.

Hyphen – punctuation mark used to join two words together (hat-trick means something different from hat trick). They are also used to show where words have been split at the ends of lines.

Inflection – the way words change their shape to show, for example, that they are singular or plural (e.g. table becomes tables) and to indicate tense (e.g. change becomes changes/changed/changing)

ing-clauses – a type of clause which contains the -ing form of a verb. For example: Walking down the street, I saw my mate Katie. It is important to make sure that the subject and the -ing verb make sense.

Minor sentence – a sentence which contains no verb. Exclamations are often minor sentences: "Never!" "Ouch!"

Singular – a word applied to nouns to show that there is only one of them, e.g. desk, computer, telephone. These are all singular. To become plural, each would gain an -s. Some words are the same in their singular and plural forms – e.g. 1 sheep, 20 sheep.

Noun – a word which labels a person, thing or idea. There are four types of noun:
common – e.g. computer, sandwich, cats
proper – e.g. Coke, Russia, Sally
abstract – e.g. death, hunger, heaven
collective – e.g. pack of dogs, flock of sheep

Paragraph – a group of sentences linked together by their theme or topic.

Phrase – a group of words which makes sense within a clause or sentence but cannot stand on its own – e.g. The old grey overcoat. My garden. Thinking carefully.

Plural – more than one.

Prefix – letters added to the beginning of a word to change its meaning (e.g. un+happy).

Preposition – a word used chiefly to show where something or someone is – for example, in, on, under. Sometimes we use 'multi-word' prepositions – ahead of, near to, in addition to.

Pronoun – a word which can be used in place of a noun – e.g. The Prime Minister visited today. Did you see him?

Punctuation – the marks we use in writing to help the reader understand our ideas. They are the written equivalent of the way we use tone of voice and pauses in speech.

Question mark – punctuation mark used to indicate that the sentence is a question. In speech, we raise the pitch of our voice at the end to show that the sentence is a question.

Register – the way we change our use of language in different situations. We might use a formal register in a school assembly ("Good morning, today I wish to discuss with you …") or an informal register with friends ("Hi, let me tell you about …")

Relative clauses – also known as wh- clauses: these are clauses that you can add to sentences to give more detail. Take a simple sentence like "My cat loves me". Add a wh- clause: "My cat, who is now ten years old, loves me".

Relative pronoun – words such as <u>who</u>, <u>which</u> and <u>that</u> used at the start of relative clauses.

Semi-colon – punctuation mark somewhere in strength between a full stop and a comma. It often replaces the word <u>and</u> between clauses and phrases.

Sentence – a group of words which can stand on their own. We expect sentences to:

★ contain a main verb
★ begin with a capital letter
★ end with a full stop, question mark or exclamation mark.

Grammar Essentials explores three sentence types: simple, compound and complex.

Singular – one.

Standard English – the most important dialect or variety of English. It is used in most written texts, in education, in law, and in the media. It is the form of English defined in dictionaries.

Subject and object – The subject is the person or thing in a sentence that is doing the action of the verb. In "Mary shouted at Kim" Mary is the subject – she is doing the shouting. The object is the person who receives the action – in this case, Kim.

Suffix – letters added to the end of a word to change its meaning – e.g. hope + less.

Tense – the form of a verb which describes when something happens (I <u>said</u> hello. I <u>say</u> hello. I <u>will say</u> hello.).

Verb – a word which tells us what someone or something is doing – e.g. she <u>saw</u> the car. It <u>slowed</u> to a standstill.

Word class – a group of words with a particular function in a sentence – nouns, verbs, adjectives, adverbs, prepositions, conjunctions, and so on.